The Developing Child:

The First Seven Years

THE GATEWAYS SERIES THREE

Compiled from articles published
in the Newsletter of the Waldorf
Early Childhood Association
of North America

The publisher wishes to acknowledge the former
and present editors of *Gateways:*
Joan Almon, Nicola Tarshis, and Stephen Spitalny.

This book is a collection of essays and articles
that originally appeared in *Gateways* and other publications.
All have been printed with the permission of the authors.

Editor: Susan Howard
Managing Editor: Lydia Roberson
Cover Art: Richard Neal
Cover Design: Dale Hushbeck
Layout and Design: Sheila Harrington
Graphics: Erica Merkling and Julie Stunden
Text Editing: Sandy Milczarek
Administrative Support: Patti Regan, Melissa Lyons and Anne Jimenez

This publication is made possible
through a grant from the Waldorf Curriculum Fund.

Published in the United States by the Waldorf Early Childhood Association of North America
285 Hungry Hollow Road, Spring Valley, NY 10977

ISBN
978-0-9796232-1-9

Table of Contents

Readiness for Kindergarten and School

Stages of Development in the First Seven Years

The Laws of Childhood

Dr. Helmut von Kügelgen

Childhood is governed by sublime laws, and demands humanity and selflessness from the adult world. For this reason, the small child poses a great challenge to our intellectual modern consciousness. Should the realm of childhood be protected from the "experts," whose thoughts are not born of love and perceptivity? Should the invasive experimentation, which alters and thereby affronts human destiny, be forbidden? Should it not still be our duty to our children to think ahead in reverence before daring to demand something of them—or before with drawing and leaving them to their own devices? No matter how we act, we form children in our own image: it is not their consciousness, or even the soul, which has not yet spread its wings to take flight, but the convolutions of the brain, the fine vibrations of the glands, liver, circulatory system that we affect.

As a result, the first law of childhood is that the small child's whole body is a sense organ, open to any and every impression. The child is extremely sensitive to the immediate surroundings. A smile, an expression of love, a tender word (unequaled sources of warmth and strength), colors, shapes, arrangement of things, and the positive thoughts of the people in the surroundings—all shape and form the child as do nervousness, senseless acts and outbursts of temper.

It is thus not so much heredity that is responsible for the similarity between parents and child; rather, small children are not yet consciously able to shield themselves from outside influences. These impressions penetrate right to the marrow of their bones—their reactions can be seen, for example, in changes in skin color or in digestive problems. The first days of a child's life, as more and more psychologists are discovering, have a lasting influence because the initial impressions grow with the child's body, as scars or as healthy tissue do.

The second law is one born of love, a sacred habit that every individual brings along: learning takes place through imitation, which incorporates the impressions made on children by their surroundings. An act of love, even if it was merely an act of sexual intercourse, summoned the child's being and prepared a body as a physical abode. From the loving spiritual world of the unborn, the child brings over a feeling of unbounded trust in the goodness of our world. Thus, there is the desire to imitate everything, and everything becomes part of the child through imitation: gestures, inner attitudes, outward conduct, language we use and the thoughts we think. "Imitation" is the magic word in the child's education until the age of nine or ten, when it is gradually replaced by other forms of learning. The child's habit of imitating us—filled with great trust and equally great expectations—exhorts us to be worthy of that imitation. Not lectures, but meaningful actions mold a "brain" which is capable of thinking meaningful thoughts. Inconsistency has the opposite effect.

These considerations lead us to the third law, which remains of great importance for the first years of schooling—and which is still a painful experience for the student struggling during exams: the forces of growth and memory (visual representation) are identical. Burdened with pedantic knowledge, children are robbed of the formative forces necessary to develop and strengthen their growing bodies. This is the reason why most precocious children look pale and wan, and why children who play imaginative games have a healthy complexion. Why should young children be weighed down with the banalities of everyday life? They will learn soon enough to differentiate between thick and thin, round and square, or between the fireman and the policeman—and will have no trouble doing so. The most important thing for the first seven years of life is to stimulate the child's creative imagination through play and actual doing.

For this age group more than for any other, the following holds true: *The child learns to be human from other human beings.* What happens if this fourth law is disregarded? If the parent or teacher replaces their own stories, games, efforts and failures with books, learning materials, or even the television set, they deprive the child of the most important thing they can give: human contact. The perception of a personality behind the activities the child sees in turn awakens the child's own personality. For what good are knowledge and more knowledge if a person has no imagination and is incapable of forming judgments and acting responsibly on those insights?

There are three different kinds of "sustenance" that nourish children and become part of them: food, the air they breathe and the sense impressions from the world around them. So, the fifth law is pay attention to quality. Prepare meals lovingly, using as many wholesome fruits and vegetables of the season as possible. An attitude of thankfulness for "our daily bread" increases its value; indifference, indulgence and lack of social graces reduce it. In the family, there should be an alternation between outside and inside activities, sleeping and waking, serious moments and times of joy, Sundays and workdays. All of these factors make an essential contribution to the quality of the sense impressions children take in from their surroundings. Should they have mechanical toys or the stones, shells, building blocks and pieces of cloth that stimulate the imagination? Should they have woolen underwear or synthetics? Is the instinctive feeling that small children do not belong in front of the television set (not even to watch programs made for children!) already dead? Strollers should be built so that children can see and be reassured by the adult's face, for exposure to a flood of impressions from the street that children cannot assimilate only serves to make them nervous. We should constantly remind ourselves that anything that children cannot digest or that is of poor quality only weakens them. Children challenge our adult world to critical reflection. From their point of view, much could indeed be said about the quality of our cities, the daily rhythm of our outer lives and the richness of our inner lives. Children demand humanity from us.

At what age do they become our contemporaries? In the beginning, they still live in mankind's earlier, dream-like state of consciousness; later, they will most certainly overtake us, for it is their task to take up the torch of the new generation. At no time, however, are they miniature adults. They must be gradually strengthened for the tasks of our century and equipped to carry its burdens. This upbringing must proceed step by step. Giving children too little of what they need for their age—or giving it to them too early—creates problems right from the start. That is why the sixth law under consideration here is: development takes time, each step being built upon the preceding one. In the first two to three years, this development proceeds by leaps and bounds. Children learn more during this time than later during job training or in the university. The will power to stand erect and to learn to walk is followed by the child's awakening to feelings that find their expression in the spoken work. Only thereafter is the first word that is thought, and not imitated, spoken: the word "I."

This three-fold development also holds true for the first seven years of child development. First, children must come to grips with gravity, testing their will with each step taken. Then, reaching beyond the outstretched hand in the form of words, they express the first stirrings of the soul. A dialogue with nature and the world of fairy tales and an exploration of the social and imaginative-artistic aspect of language has begun. Finally (between the ages of five and seven), uniting word and language gestures, the child forms the first thoughts, creates new words and philosophies as only a child can. This law is clearly shown again in the three seven-year periods leading up to adulthood. Up to school age, and somewhat beyond, children should do things in order to grasp them, learning through play and their own experience. Up to puberty, they should learn both through experiencing things and through discussions. What has been learned is no longer incorporated, instead, feelings slowly begin to take wing. During puberty, lively interest in people's destinies, both near and far, should develop, expanding their horizon beyond their own country. Only now, on the basis of their own many varied experiences, can young people begin to form their own judgments. At this point, they have crossed the threshold from childhood to youth. A love of truth, science, and self-chosen responsibilities and obligations and an urge to act on their own insights, become strong, leading to career decisions and adulthood. Now the task is to think before one acts. Willing and thinking—after a strengthening of their intermediary, feeling—have entered into a new relationship with one another.

What is already present in small children grows with them as they mature. So the final law is to protect childhood. Shield it from experimentation, from premature development, from floods of stimuli, from everything that serves to weaken the child's powers of imagination. Protect childhood as a source of physical well being, of inner strength, of self-identity, of social tolerance. If childhood is not filled with joy and warmth, imaginative games and meaningful experiences, many obstacles are placed in the path of sound development.

⁓

Dr. Helmut von Kügelgen spent thirty years as a teacher at the original Waldorf school in Stuttgart and was the founder of the International Association of Waldorf Kindergartens. He also served as Director of the Waldorf Kindergarten Seminar in Stuttgart and edited a collection of booklets on the festivals and the inner life of Waldorf teachers, now available in English as the Little Series.

Stages of Development In Early Childhood: Tasks and Goals for Parents and Educators

Freya Jaffke

To be able to foster a child's development rather than disturb or hinder it through faulty behavior, we must become familiar with and understand these stages of development. This is based fact by anatomical research that a child's body inherited from her parents does not represent a smaller form of the adult. The child's body is being metamorphosed toward its own goal. One can clearly see that a Will, an individuality, is at work here which is not identical to the body that has been inherited. Three different stages of development during the years before a child is ready for first grade, up to the seventh year, are described in *Soul Economy and Waldorf Education*, Lecture VII, (Rudolf Steiner, Anthroposophic Press, 1986).

Steiner observed that the human organism is divided into three areas. Since the sense perceptions are conducted through the nerve system to the brain, Steiner calls this association of functions centered in the head the *nerve-sense system*. It is the physical basis for thinking. A second larger area consists of the connection between the rhythm of breathing and the heartbeat, in whose subtle variations the feeling life is manifested. It is called the *rhythmic system* and has its center in the chest area. The organs of metabolism perform their work deep in the unconscious. If their activity is injured, then the human will is weakened or even disabled. In no other area does the will impulse live more fully and with greater strength than in the movement of the limbs—the spontaneous, willful joy of movement in small children is a good example of this. Thus Steiner combines this "lower" region and calls it the *limb-metabolic system*.

The life processes of the organism and its formation cannot be adequately explained by the chemical reactions of body substances. Expert anthropologists acknowledge the workings of formative forces. Rudolf Steiner calls them the *formative or life forces*. Their effects in the shaping of the organism and in the physiological processes are evident. However, what exactly is at work is invisible to the external eye and is revealed only through "supersensible" methods of observation, as Steiner describes in the Fourth and Fifth Lectures of *Soul Economy*. He describes how the formative forces are completely occupied at the beginning of human life with the forming of the organism. Then, as the organs draw nearer to their final form, these forces are gradually freed up from this task and metamorphose then into spirit-soul forces: those of memory, imagination, fantasy and the power of thought. They all point to a spiritual shaping and forming. Thus childhood development consists essentially in the birth and gradual unfolding of these forces.

If we wish to understand a child in the first seven years of life, we must look very closely at the individual steps of development. Before we do this though, let us keep in mind the whole situation of the small child at the beginning of life.

To begin with, three things must coincide if a birth is to happen. First the two streams of inheritance from the parents unite to give the body. A soul-spirit being, a human individuality, then joins with the body.

For instance, in spite of its outer completeness, this physical body still remains unfinished in many ways. The individual inner organs have not yet attained their final, differentiated form. In the limb system, we see a lack of differentiation—chaotic, involuntary movements. In the nerve-sense system, the child is still totally open.

The child's task in the first six to seven years —years that are his by right for this purpose—is to take hold of his inner body and to develop its differentiation until he is ready for school. Then, when the process of forming the organs is largely finished and only growth is still taking place, his body stands prepared as a useful "instrument." The soul-spirit individuality that had joined the physical body at birth can, after further steps of development, begin to manifest itself fully in an external way through this body without being hindered by it.

How can we observe the joining of the individuality to the body? We see how the child's involuntary movements of kicking about gradually become more ordered and directed through his tireless will to be active. We see how he acquires the upright position and how he develops a relationship to the world's equilibrium in learning to walk. We observe how from the worldwide language of babbling a small child finds his way ever more surely and with greater control to the exact sound of his regional language. We see how more strongly differentiated and meaningful activity develops from the early toddling

about after adults and the beginning imitation of their behavior.

We can see through all of these processes how the individuality is endeavoring to work itself into the body and to make the body its own. All of the impressions from the environment that meet the child also work very closely in this process of shaping the inner human being. The impressions work into the child from the outside through the senses. In the small child, these are digested inwardly by the core of his being, the individuality, in two ways: through the imitated behavior and in the development of the yet unfinished organs.

The small child is born unprotected into its new environment. His whole body acts as a single sense organ serving in an indiscriminate way to join the outer world with the inner one. We can compare it to the eye. The eye itself does not se—it only transmits. We see through the eyes. Thus, the child's body is a sense organ for the individuality, for the spirit-soul being of the human.

The outer impressions come into the child through the senses, while the inner activity of shaping the organs moves outwards. This working together of the outer impressions and the inner shaping manifests itself in that wonderful power of imitation with which each healthy child is born. Every observation is first taken in deeply, grasped by the will and then, like an echo, comes forth again in a child's behavior.

The results from this fact are two significant tasks for parents and educators. The first is a gesture of protection. Wherever we are able to do so, we need to choose carefully out of the environment the impressions that meet the child. It is best if calm, happy family sounds of normal speaking and singing surround the child rather than those of uproar and quarreling. We also must protect the child from every type of technical apparatus such as radio, television, cassettes, videos, etc. In a child's room, cradles and walls of one, soft color is preferable because of the sooth- ing effect, to the well-meant children's fabrics and wallpaper that are covered with flowers and animals. When riding in the car make sure that the child can be seated to have a view of mother rather than over-stimulating the senses by expos- ing him to the street traffic.

The second great task consists in guiding the child step by step into life, allowing him to learn about life for his whole life. This happens chiefly by meaningfully and methodically paying atten- tion to the capability that the child has brought with him—that of imitation—rather than by means of clever teaching.

This presupposes that when we as grown-ups make the effort to be good "examples" of human beings, that we will have the effect of awakening impulses in the child through our activities—we cannot teach a child to imitate. This is a matter of the will and must be grasped by the child's own will. We can be aware of our own behav- ior: how we go about our work in the home and garden, how we speak with other people, how we care for others, how we arrange and care for our environment. The child takes everything deeply into his own bodily formative processes. Without being able to discriminate between meaningful or foolish behavior, he brings to his own activity what he sees in his representatives of life, which is the role we take on in the process of education.

The imitative behavior of the child goes through three different stages in the first six to seven years. It is subject to the forces forming the organs, which, beginning in the head area, work through the whole body right down to the tips of the toes. Although they work through the whole body, they concentrate in the first stage of life, from birth to about two and a half years of age, on the forming of the organs in the Nerve-Sense System. During this time the child acquires three of the most important human ca- pabilities: gaining uprightness in the face of grav- ity; walking; and then speech, which is a prereq- uisite for thinking. All of these capabilities the

child learns exclusively through imitation. Tragic examples in history have shown that children do not acquire these human capabilities when they grow up surrounded only by animals. This shows clearly that humanity can only be learned from human beings.

From the Age of Crawling to the Awakening of the "I" in the Age of Independence

In what way are children active in this first stage of life?

As soon as the child can barely crawl or propel himself forward, he begins to explore his home environment, and it becomes unsafe. He follows Mother and wants to do everything that she is doing. With the greatest enjoyment he clatters together the cooking pots, covers and spoons, puts his hands into the wash water, pulls out the wash and sticks it in again, spreading puddles about. He bustles about with the broom, dispersing the dirt rather than gathering it into the middle in a small pile; he eagerly carries things that have just been placed in a certain spot to some other spot. And all this is done with the motto, "Johnny, too" or "Me, too!" He takes great joy in moving and busying himself as much as possible with real household items, yet without insight into the purpose and goal of the adult's work , which, of course, progresses very slowly. Without such "willing helpers," the adult work would be done much sooner. How- ever, this is true only from one point of view, for the parent has taken care not only of the house, garden or handwork, but at the same time she has also accomplished educational work. This should become recognized in today's educational awareness.

Along with impulsive engagement with the environment, there are also moments when the child lingers devotedly near Mother, for example, when she is peeling apples or working with nee- dle and thread. There are times when she busies herself in the play area, filling up baskets and emptying them, building towers and knocking them down, singing and pushing a doll carriage. Here it is important to pay close attention to the quality of the play materials. The best objects are those found in nature or which have been only slightly shaped by hand, (*Toymaking with Children*, Jaffke, 1988). In her close connection with these objects, the impressions made upon the child will be natural, organic shapes, and this works to stimulate her inner organ forming processes. "Toys with dead mathematical forms alone have a desolating and killing effect upon a child's formative forces." (*The Education of the Child*, Rudolf Steiner)

The child passes through a first real crisis point when for the first time the feeling of "I" is awakened during the Age of Defiance. He experiences his own will more and more, but must now learn to bring it into harmony with his environment. Whereas earlier, he always called out "Me, too," now he says, "I don't want to."

From the Third to the Fifth Year: Fantasy and Spontaneous Play

Let us now take a look at the second stage, the time between about the third to fifth year. The life or formative forces, which until now have chiefly been at work in the head region, concentrate in this second stage in the middle part of the body, where most importantly the rhythmical organs (heart and lungs) are located. At this time, two quite new capabilities appear in the child, which clearly give him a new relationship to his environment. These capabilities are a childlike fantasy and memory.

Here are some examples of play in children who have developed in a healthy way:

- A four-year-old boy has small round pieces of real tree branches in front of him on the table, and he asks me, "Do you want soda, beer or apple juice?"

- A four-year-old girl takes a piece of bark, lays two stones upon it and says, "I have a ship

with a man at the wheel." Then she comes to my table and asks, "I have brought you some pieces of chocolate, do you want them?" and she lays the stones in front of me. Then the bark becomes a roof for a small dwarf's house.

- A small bench was first a doll's stove, then became an animal's feeding trough when laid on its side, and, upside down it was first a doll's bed and then part of a train.

These examples show that children of this age are capable of changing things in their environment, using them for different purposes in certain cases and with the help of fantasy making them into new things. Children see objects, perhaps remembering them only vaguely, and their imagination fills in all the other necessary details. The prerequisite is that children have already experienced such things before. If a child has never seen a ship, or only saw one in a picture book, he cannot bring it into his play.

A characteristic of play at this age is that it is stimulated by external causes. For this reason, it is best if the available play materials are capable of transformation by being incomplete and simple enough so that a child's imagination, remembering the details, can transcend the available objects and fill them in. The imagination needs this type of activity in order not to become stagnant. Everything depends on the inner work.

"As the muscles of the hand grow firm and strong in performing the work for which they are fitted, so the brain and other organs of the human physical body are guided into the right lines of development if they receive the right impression from the environment." (*Education of the Child*, Rudolf Steiner)

It is immediately striking that the play is full of change. There are always daily events that are imitated, and there are many spontaneous changes, often without any connection. Children continuously think of something new. Many adults who see this may despair and believe the children are unable to concentrate in their play. Concentration at this age level, however, lies in the continuity of play which, between three and five years of age, is characterized in this way. To be sure, quite a bit of disorder and even chaos arises now and then from this play, but it can be called meaningful chaos for it continuously affects the children in such a way that they remain stimulated and interested. By the fifth year, this already changes on its own. Of course, after playtime, the adult plans sufficient time to clean up, participating herself to set an example so that it becomes an indisputable and joyful habit rather than a sporadically ordered, almost overwhelming burden which one faces alone.

From the Fifth to the Seventh Year: Pictures from the Imagination and Planned Play

The third big developmental step of the first seven years begins around the fifth year. The forces that have been used to form the organs are being freed more and more from the rhythmical system and are now working in the metabolic-limb system. Children become increasingly capable and dexterous right down to their fingertips.

Many children, especially those who were able to play in a rich and creative manner, go through a second crisis in the fifth year. For the first time, they experience a real boredom. A child can stand before you and say, "I don't know what to do." It is as if her fantasy has left her and suddenly she has no more ideas. The fantasy needs a rest now and should not be called upon by reminding the child of yesterday's fine play. We can help to strengthen it much more by having the child participate in our own work, for example, peeling apples, drying dishes, sweeping, baking, sewing. After a while, sometimes after only a few days, new impulses for play arise in the child. A change has taken place. The stimulus for play no longer comes so much from external objects, but it comes now more and more from inside. This means that now the child has

an inner picture, a picture from her imagination of past events, and she can bring these up in her play independent of place, time or people.

Five- and six-year-old children love to sit together talking and making plans for their play. For example, they are building an inn, and folded cloths become napkins, menus and purses. A cold buffet is set up, and little woolen sheep are offered as fish. One child, who is selling drinks, has a large log with small branches on it standing before him (it is his "real beer keg"), and he is able to fill an order for any kind of drink. Another time, they set up a doctor's office with needles, stethoscopes, bandages and a waiting room where the folded cloths serve as magazines.

Other typical themes of play are: trash truck, ambulance with a red light, school, carpentry shop, fire engine, cable-railway, telephone installation, deep sea diver and much more. Their play becomes more and more planned. This does not mean, however, that it can't be suddenly changed in the middle if one of the children comes up with a rousing idea.

Children of this age do not need fancier, more detailed playthings. Play materials that can grow with them are better. Their relationship to the materials is changing. Before the fifth year, the materials stimulate ideas. After the fifth year, an imaginative idea comes first, then comes an effort to find and make something acceptable from the play materials that corresponds to the imagination. Now the fantasy, which had been so richly developed before, begins to function again.

Nowadays, it is no longer a matter of course that children can play so spontaneously and enthusiastically at their corresponding level of development. This is due less to the children than to the immense influence from all sides upon them from earliest childhood on. For example, fully detailed, technically exact toys make it difficult for children to be satisfied with such outwardly simple things as objects from nature, cloths, wooden branches, etc. A healthy child would rather be right in the middle of play, than outside as an observer of perfect, technical instruments. The fascination for such toys is soon past and leaves behind an emptiness and longing for more.

One of our most important tasks is to arrange the space—at home and in the kindergarten—to guarantee the needs of creative play. Above all, this means creating a world suitable for imitation with adults who are active in a purposeful way, who like to do their work, and who, at the same time, accompany the children in their play in a quiet way. Creative play depends more on a calm, joyful atmosphere of work than on many clever words, suggestions for play or instructions of any kind. The children must be "lifted up" by the adults' work; they must have a place in it in the broadest sense, even if they are not directly involved in the work. This seems like a contradiction, but it can be experienced by every mother who brings her mending basket or ironing board to the children's room and who radiates calm and interest while working, or by every father who goes about his work in the garden, yard or cellar. The most important thing is that the people who surround the child make life rhythmical and orderly, that they like to work and are ready to take on a large part of the work themselves. The small child is an imitator!

The unspoken reward and thanks for such efforts come to the adult through children who are able to play in a fulfilling way and who are building the basis for later life in these early stages.

In retrospect, the tasks of the educator can easily be discovered from all of the above descriptions. We can summarize the goals in this way. The most wonderful thing that can happen in childhood is that the child is able to grasp completely each developmental step and pass through it in a healthy way, and that he is able to practice and gain strength during each particular challenge. When the body is completely formed and accomplishes its first change around age seven, the child may turn to his schoolwork with the same joy, strength and enthusiasm for learning that he showed earlier for play and be equal to its demands.

❧

Freya Jaffke is now retired after many decades of work as a Waldorf kindergarten teacher in southern Germany. She continues to be active in adult education and lectures widely throughout the world. Her books on early childhood have sold over a quarter of a million copies worldwide.

The Young Child from Birth to Seven

Dennis Klocek

I would like to address a difficult subject in the work of Rudolf Steiner. We could say it is the question: What is the etheric? This is a difficult question because the birth of a child into the world, the birth of the physical body of a child, is accompanied by etheric forces from the cosmos that have been working through nine months to form a kind of cupola, a space, into which all of the patterns of organs and endocrine pathways, warmth and cold differentials, membranes, secretions—all of these very complex chemical reactions—have to be somehow coordinated and integrated in one space, with very little room for error. If we really think of the miracle of organization that it takes to bring an embryo to term, it is mind-boggling. Yet it is a daily occurrence. We look at this great miracle and almost take it for granted.

That process of the becoming of the human being from the nothing to the something is spearheaded and supported by the forces of the etheric. The whole being of the embryo is surrounded by cosmic Ego forces—forces of destiny, karma, heredity, entering a particular race, and incarnating into a particular geographic area. All of those forces are a kind of filter very far out in the cosmos, which we could call the *Ego principle*. The Ego could be thought of as a lens, but it is a selective lens that brings certain forces from the cosmos to bear into a center. It brings

forces from the periphery and integrates them into what we could call a relative center. It does that primarily through the gates of the senses. The forming of the sense life in the environment of the embryo is really orchestrated by what later will be called the ego organization from the physical side or, from a cosmic side, the true self. The ego organization in the embryo is the actual physical response of matter to the organizing forces of the cosmos, but those physical responses are based on patterns of sensation that exist in potential in the farthest reaches of the cosmos. We could say that sensation is the raw material of the cosmos. No physiologist can really explain sensation in a mechanical, chemical model. Even though we know all of the instruments and the pathways that sensation takes in physiology, when it comes to the question in embryology of just how sensation forms the embryo, no one knows, but most agree that sensation does form the embryo.

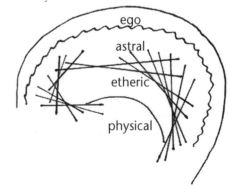

I recently read an article in the *Sacramento Bee* about a new thesis that, yes, neurons do grow. For many years it has been assumed that the human being comes in with a certain complement of neurons, and that's it for the rest of life. It has been discovered that in songbirds, part of the brain actually atrophies every season so that a new song can be learned. It was considered that a human being already had a full complement of neurons and that new neuronal patterns could not be developed. The researcher who determined that twenty years ago has now reversed his position. He now says, yes indeed, new neurons can be developed, even to old age, but it depends on the effects of the environment. This is cutting edge research, and this is exactly what Rudolf Steiner was saying years ago.

We could say that the Ego acts, through the gates of the twelve senses, as a kind of filter or lens for cosmic force. Inside that gate of the senses within the organism is found the action of the "cosmic astral body, the motion of the planets—in front of the fixed stars—creating loops, pockets, angles, and particular forms. Within that realm of the cosmic astral is what we could call the personal etheric, or the individualized etheric. It is these individualized etheric forces to which Rudolf Steiner is often referring when he uses the phrase *etheric formative forces*. They are the etheric forces, which create form. The etheric forces themselves, per se, are really cosmic forces. According to Rudolf Steiner, if the human form were placed into the pure, cosmic etheric forces, it would be disintegrated; it would be annihilated.

Now this seems like a contradictory perspective that in one instance the etheric forces would annihilate the human form, and from another perspective the etheric forces are there as the source of the sculptural forces, of the building of the form. It seems contradictory, until we develop a perspective that every "body" such as the Ego, the astral body, the etheric body—every subtle body—has a cosmic dimension and

an earthly dimension. In the earthly dimension, these cosmic forces, which really live on the periphery of the cosmos, come under the spell, so to speak, of the Ego being and become focused into a relative center. From there these cosmic forces begin to create form. They begin to create the possibility of the upbuilding and maintaining of the form. The upbuilding of the form is the work of the musical forces.

The musical forces allow the *new* to have a place to manifest. The creation of the previously determined pattern of the form itself and its decay, we could say, are the work of the etheric forces. It is when the cosmic side of these celestial forces comes under the sway of an Ego being that the possibility of awakening in a body of flesh arises. The young child exists as a spiritual being—living among spiritual beings as a cosmic Ego—and starts a journey through the stars and the planets, picking up impulses from the stars and planets that will eventually become the actual functions and forms within the human body. Human beings are on a journey toward incarnation. They take these celestial forces and, through the deeds of Lucifer and Ahriman, focus these celestial forces in a relative center to such a degree that an illusion of a separate self arises and is sustained.

This does not mean that the incarnated being no longer has a transcendent cosmic self. It just means that the illusion of the separate self has become so focused by the Ego being that the adversaries have gained access to it through the door of matter. The matter gets incorporated into these celestial forces as an image of particular regions of the cosmos in the lungs, the liver, the kidneys, the heart, the bones, the senses, and all of the interaction between the life organs and the sense organs. This all gives the human being the possibility of becoming another small universe. The potential human has a full complement of cosmic forces, but they have been individualized to the degree that the being who is occupying this new body has the distinct impression that he or she is the center of the universe.

There is nothing wrong with this except that the original plan was that, as soon as this perception arose, the human being would immediately have the complementary perception that our intrinsic uniqueness is what we have in common with every other being that says "I." According to Rudolf Steiner, that was the original plan. The function of a human being was to oscillate between those two states of consciousness as a kind of reciprocating relief valve between the cosmos and the Earth, to allow for a breathing between a peripheral cosmos and a centric cosmos. The ether body of the child, under the influence of the incarnating Ego at the physical birth, becomes a kind of lens or focalizing agent that takes part of the cosmic ether—the stars we could say, or the light of the stars—and gathers the qualities of earth, water, air, and fire that exist in the various constellations. As the sun moves through the zodiac, it brings, month by month, the successive qualities of earth, water, air, and fire into the ethers around the earth. The incarnating Ego, which is an image of the sun moving through the cosmos, focuses into a relative center in the embryo a field of forces that the embryo participates in for nine months. The other three months that are left over, we could say, are the reason why we come back because we can't really have the whole picture of the whole cosmos in one incarnation. Then when we do come back, we will have another three points of view we haven't quite worked out for each incarnation.

The activity of the Ego that brings a whole starry realm into focus, also brings a focus into the other subtle bodies. In the other subtle bodies, the individualized etheric forces could be called earthly etheric forces, or personal etheric forces. Those personal etheric forces have the property of being plant-like. Plants have two fundamental modes of action: they grow and then they decay. Growth and decay are the properties

of life. Life grows by adding one and adding one and adding one. That is growth. The paradox is that life also decays by adding one and adding one and adding one. This is because if we keep adding and adding and adding, suddenly the physical dimensions of the being exceed its ability to maintain the integrity of the life.

This is called the law of minimal surfaces in physics. What it means is, if something gets too big, it has to get broken apart. Think of a balloon. We fill a balloon; we keep filling and filling a balloon. As we keep filling the balloon, we're just filling the balloon. We're doing the same thing; we are growing. But suddenly something happens. As the mass of the being grows by cubes (three dimensions), the surface is only growing by squares (two dimensions), and something has got to give. The surface membrane ruptures, and the organism goes back to a more economical stage; the organism forms a committee. Instead of trying to solve everything in the College of Teachers, we form committees, and we mandate them to grow. It is exactly the same process. All that is happening in the social life is the law of minimal surfaces.

In the biological sphere, this limits the size of the growth of a particular cell. The cell of an elephant or a whale is the same size as the cell of a mouse; there is no difference. There are just more of them. The size of a cell is limited by its ability to maintain integrity between the center of the cell and the periphery of the cell. This is the image of the Thrones (the Spirits of Will), the Kyriotetes, and the Spirits of Motion. There is just so much growth that can happen inside a cell, until the membrane has to rupture, and then the cell goes through a process to reform into a smaller size, as two cells. There you have the Exusiai. Then the cell can maintain integrity. These are images that we could call the laws of the etheric, and they govern everything from individual cells in your body to governments and social revolutions. They are images of the same principles, and they come from the first phase of evolution on Old Saturn. In Rudolf Steiner's teachings, the etheric forces have two parameters. They bring life forces, forces of growth, from the periphery.

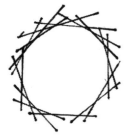 

In the diagram above, I've drawn a circle, made of lines, that represents what Rudolf Steiner calls the planar forces of the etheric realm. He says that the ether forces come to the organism as planes of light from the periphery. The life comes to the organism from the periphery, from the cosmos. The growth also comes to the organism from the periphery. But within the transformed ether body of etheric formative forces, these growth forces have become so individualized that they link themselves up to the physical properties of the matter that gets incorporated into them. What results from the originally cosmic growth forces is that suddenly matter falls out of the now individualized growth forces, like the wake of a ship. There is a kind of turbulence. As the growth forces form a space, matter goes into the space and fills it up. Then what is left is matter, and the growth forces withdraw to the periphery to create another layer of life in which matter can manifest. This is the way a tree grows from the cambium. The cambium is on the periphery; that is where the life is.

In the human organism, on the periphery are the senses: seeing, hearing, tasting, and touching. The life forces—through the senses, through the sensation—come into the young child from the periphery—starlight pouring through the gates of the senses. This is cosmic life. The forces, cosmic life, form the organs in cosmic star patterns of earth, water, air, and fire; they form the lung, liver, kidney, and heart. The particular pattern of the particular organ is a picture of the way in which the elements are working in that particular realm. The lung is a picture of the earth, the way in which the carbon of the earth unites with substances and then dissolves, for instance. These life forces from the periphery come in contact with young children through the environment, through what they hear, see, touch, and taste. The moods of the adults around the children also carry these life forces in the their sheaths. Young children have a kind of atavistic clairvoyance as to how humans or animals have organized these cosmic forces. They don't listen so much to the content of a speaker's voice but to the intent, to the elemental mood of the speaker. They look at the way in which the curves in the speaker's face are animated or not, the way in which their limbs reflect their inner mobility, and from there the children build their own organs from birth to seven. This is an enormous thought, that what is in the environment of a child from birth to seven is what is actually forming her life organs, through the gates of the senses. These life organs are nourished by sense impressions from the environment.

Now, in the child from birth to seven, the physical body has been born and the ether body has been pulled by the Ego into the physical body, but the ether body hasn't yet been freed. It is still working in a rather cosmic way. It is gestating, we could say, in the child from birth to seven. It is mulling over the impressions, the life impressions, that are coming in, and forming the inner organs according to the dictates of the cosmos: Now you must form a liver. Now you must form a lung. Now you must form a heart. We could think that those organs are created in the embryo and finished, but no. They are seed-like in the fetus that has come to term and are still unfolding. They need earth evolution in order to actually experience how the cosmic ether forces have come through the realm of the planets and are actually forming and creating the earthly forms of the body. This process is an initiation that young children go through before the change of teeth so that, later on, when they pick up their karma-designated temperament, when the ether body is born, they will be able to take a particular temperament on for a time and then let go of it in order to integrate it into the other temperaments. They need to have an initiation into the school of the elemental beings.

musical and sculptural forces co-operate

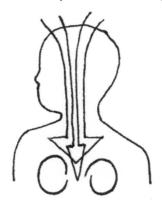

The elemental initiation the child has is the forming of his life organs as a gestation process in the period from birth to seven. That initiation is through the sensations that they receive from their environment. As a result, their educative principle is imitation. They imitate what is in the environment around them. Teaching through example is the most effective form of education for birth to seven, because this is the biological imperative of that age. The etheric formative forces are impacting the physical being directly. There is no other type of cognition going on, aside from the fact that the cosmos is working to gestate an ether body. The sensations that the children experience are nutrition for their life organs directly.

Now, in the diagram here, I have tried to show a child from birth to seven, and Rudolf Steiner, in *Balance in Teaching*, gives a very interesting picture.

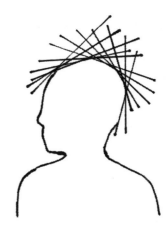

Rudolf Steiner says that the head principle is the area where there is a receiving of these cosmic life forces. It is because the head is really where the gateway to the senses is most concentrated. Through hearing and seeing, mainly, there is an influx, a constant influx, of these cosmic ether forces under the activity of the Ego that is united with them. A part of the cosmic ego is building the Ego organization, which is what will eventually be the instrument and life forces of the partially incarnated cosmic Ego. The ego organization is being built by this cosmic Ego, or true self, by uniting itself with part of the etheric formative forces and bringing them into contact with the physical. There is a kind of drawing down that the true self does; it focuses the ether forces down into the physical. As that happens, the activity is primarily focused in the head region. So the birth-to-seven child has a very large head because that, as we could say in a kind of funny way, is its antenna, because the antenna is resonant to the signal, and the signal is from the cosmos. This is what enables the child to draw in cosmic forces through the gates of the senses. They are focalized in the head, an image of the cosmos.

The cosmic forces come into the head, pour down from the head, and into the rest of the body. They are not there in the way they are in the older child, because in the young child the ego has only partially incarnated into the etheric forces. The etheric forces are not yet freed because the ether body has not yet been born, but they are there working to make the life organs and to complete their forming. So the picture is this: the cosmos works through the senses from the periphery, forming them in a very cosmic way. Hidden in the music, the speech, and in what is seen in the environment of the child are forces that are building, forming, structuring. In addition to that, these etheric forces that come in contact with the earthly forces are also destroying and decaying, because the ether body, as we have said, is plant-like. The plant grows and decays; that is what it does.

Now we come to one of the difficult parts in *Balance in Teaching*, where Rudolf Steiner gives the picture that the astral body, through the musical forces, creates the processes that he calls upbuilding. In other places, he will say that the astral body is the source of illness, which can seem contradictory. We have to be very precise as we use these terms because they are really not contradictory at all. These concepts just require saying beforehand: This is what I am talking about at this particular stage.

In the birth-to-seven child, the ether body—the gestating ether body—dominates. The physical body is built according to that gestation pattern, but there is a kind of turbulence in the gestation. It is just like the experience women have who have given birth; there is a bit of turbulence that comes into life during that period. It is the same in the birth-to-seven child. There is turbulence in the body that is being gestated—we could say etheric turbulence. That etheric turbulence manifests itself in the oscillation between, *"Yes, I am like an angel,"* and *"Now, I am less like an angel,"* that goes on between birth and seven—sometimes overnight, sometimes day to day, sometimes hour to hour. The oscillation moves back and forth between the more dynamic cosmic forces and some very incarnated fixed habit patterns. This is because the ether body, when it falls to earth and becomes earthly, is the source of habit. When these patterns later become free, at the birth of the etheric, they will

be the source of temperament. The temperament, then, becomes a problem for the Ego, because the ether forces in it are fixed through habit and may not still have access to the cosmic patterns that are needed to maintain the organism. When we want to change a habit, it is very difficult to do that because the ether body, very early, is formed by particular patterns of sensation. The earthly forces that are given to this young being in the sensations in the environment form patterns in the life organs, which go on and later become temperamental disposition.

There is a picture of this that I have found to be very useful—the difference between a suspension and a solution. If we try to understand the activity of the etheric formative forces, we can think in terms of what a suspension is. In a suspension, there is matter suspended in a fluid medium. No matter how fine the matter becomes even after repeated pulverization, if we let that sit for a while, the matter will eventually fall out of suspension and become a precipitate at the bottom of the vessel. This is the oscillation between form and decay. When a being is coming into manifestation, it uses the peripheral forces as a kind of forming blueprint or template. Those form-forces are pure life and have not yet attracted matter. That is the role of water. But then, through continued forming and the action of the Ego focused on a relative center, matter is drawn in and gets formed into substance. Once matter gets formed, it comes under the laws of the earth. It starts to build and open up, and then, due to the law of minimal surfaces, the membrane at the periphery is disrupted, followed by the breakdown of the systems. The system that has been formed breaks down into smaller and smaller pieces. This is decay—the pieces go back to earth. In the language of alchemy, this is called a "salt process." The salt goes into apparent solution and is lifted into a levity state by the water, and then the water evapoartes, and the salt comes back out again just as it went in. Chemically, that is a suspension. In a true solution, the salt would never come back out of the liquid. The salt, never falling again, would be the activity of musical forces. This is what Rudolf Steiner calls, "upbuilding"—what we could call cooking. In order to do that, matter has to be taken to a higher and higher level of levity.

These images are useful when we try to imagine the disposition of a child, the mood of a child, from birth to seven. As educators, what could we really look for? Even though there is not a temperamental response yet because the temperaments have not actually formed, there is the beginning of a temperamental response in the forming of a particular organ in the preschooler. This first temperamental blush is given by the organ in the body that looks after life—the liver.

The liver is connected most directly to the ether forces of forming and decaying, of coming into being and then going away—this is the life of the liver. In the fetus, the liver and the thymus are by far the most dominant metabolic organs in the body for the whole pre-natal development. If you look in the biological evolution of the lower kingdoms for an animal which is mostly liver, you have to go through a lot of phyla until you get up to the crustaceans. The first animal in which the whole body cavity is almost completely filled with a liver is a crayfish. The characteristic life gesture of the crayfish is: Now I'm growing; now I'm hiding. It continues to grow, and it gets so big that the law of minimal surfaces takes over. The skin splits, and this very succulent little being comes out of the split skin and finds a hole to crawl into, until it can form another shell so that it is not so tasty. So there is a growth side, a developmental side, and then a sort of, "I'm shutting down and going in to my little hole" side. This is the liver rhythm, which is a picture of the sun, even though the liver is related to Jupiter. The sun rhythm is of day and night; this is decaying (day)-growing (night).

What we could call the liver mood, or even the crayfish mood, is the source of the mood oscillations of the young child. She is sweet, lovely, delicate, and gentle, and then she turns around and whacks her baby brother in the head with their doll. And you wonder, "How can this be?" When the liver dominates the consciousness, there is tremendous growth and then a complete shutting down, going within, resting, and covering one's head—one could even say there is a depression. If these forces are not met and harmonized from birth to seven, if there is not a daily rhythm, then the liver, in adulthood, will be trying to return to a stage of development where it can find in its environment forces which allow it to approach its cosmic archetype. It will be searching for rhythmic forces in its environment that allow it to once again get in contact with its life. Unless this is developed and nurtured in the environment of the child from birth to seven, then the liver mood will permeate the rest of the temperamental development in the lower school, and then really erupt in high school, and then become depression in intellectual soul times.

This is the root of depression. Depression really is a kind of hunger for rhythmic sensation, for sensation which is non-threatening and which can be assimilated or, we could even say, digested into life. As educators, we need to be careful that strong sensation doesn't come so quickly that the child can not digest it. Sensation should also not move abstractly into concepts for the young child, for as soon as young children are challenged with abstract ideas, there is kind of shell that forms around their life forces. Even in adults this happens. So the pictures, movements, and sounds in the environment of the child from birth to seven need to be rhythmically presented with a very keen perception of day to night, and season to season, because it is that kind of etheric, rhythmic force that the liver is listening to as a kind of cosmic digestion of sensation.

In his physiology lectures, Rudolf Steiner gives a picture of the liver as an organ that is an arrested head formation. When you first read that you say, "What does that mean?" If we look at the picture that I presented earlier of the head receiving cosmic forces through sensation, and we look at the liver and its place in biology, the liver comes out in the embryo as a bud of the digestive system and begins to function, receiving impulses from the world through the digested food that comes out of the intestines and the lymph. It is, we could say, listening to the sensations of the world in those fluids. The liver sits amid all of that lymph with all of these foodstuffs, and gathers it in. Into that sea of lymph there are tremendous sensations that are playing up through the lymph fluids based on the patterns of sensation in the sympathetic nervous system in the child. Rudolf Steiner connects the sympathetic nervous system to the etheric body, and it is in that ether body that shocks to the system are registered. The sympathetic nervous system brings balance back into a system that has been overloaded, stressed, or shocked. So the sympathetic nervous system, especially in the metabolic system, is connected to the movements of the limbs. It reacts to jerking movements in sensations, abruptness, hardness, coarseness; these all register in the physiology of the child, especially in the metabolic organs, as a kind of etheric disturbance. The metabolic system then has to secrete into the lymph all kinds of reactive secretions that cause the liver to say: "What's that? Is this okay? Is this all right? Something's going wrong!"

The liver, we could say, becomes harried. It is constantly thinking that something is wrong. What it should be thinking is: "I wonder what is happening on Jupiter today?" That is what the liver is expecting. If it doesn't get Jupiter, if it gets simply that the adrenals and the sympathetic nervous system are dumping secretions that are a stimulus and response to environmental stress, then the liver incorporates that stress in the forming of the proteins, because the liver is a life-formative etheric organ. Because it is an etheric organ, it is a sculptural organ. What it is sculpting is the proteins that will later become liver, lung, kidney, and heart, etc. It does so by listening to the cosmic music and then sculpt-

ing the substances that come to it into usable forms for that particular physiology. So, in a way, it is like an arrested head. What it is listening to is the music of the spheres. It uses that music to create little images of Jupiter (liver), Saturn (bones), and Venus (kidney) in the body. So in *Balance in Teaching* and in various other places, Rudolf Steiner speaks of the liver as a characteristic organ that really needs to be thought about by the kindergarten teacher. The whole physiology and the whole inner life of soul that the child from birth to seven is bringing to Earth is based on an inner clairvoyance as to what is going on in the secretions of the fluids in the body.

The Ego moves in toward the incarnating child. In his inner life the child begins having memories of living among the stars. The environment impacts the senses. He is dimly aware, but not consciously aware, of how the environmental sensations come into and are reflected by the physical body. The environmental sensations bounce back up into the cosmic astral because the ether body is very flexible and fluid. The music of the spheres and the cosmic astral says, "I don't know what this is; you take it!" and reflects the personalized environmental sense patterns back down to the etheric, and suddenly the ether body is caught in an oscillation between the cosmic astral and the physical body.

The ether body doesn't know what to do with the personalized forces. So what it does is make a little moving model of this oscillating movement. This model is then called adrenaline, testosterone, thyroid secretion, or digestive juices. Bodily secretions are a kind of fixed movement model of the stimulus response pattern—one part per million of adrenaline in the blood coming out of the kidneys, and instantly the whole body is on a fight-or-flight pattern for fifteen minutes. The secretion is an individualized movement—it is a substance that is a concentrated cosmic movement. The child from birth to seven is acting out the patterns of its secretions. This is what Rudolf Steiner is saying—the

20

environment impacts the organs. The life organ tries to accommodate the personalized sensation, but the best way it does that is by creating secretion, an image of a creative movement, the secretion as movement image then goes into the blood. The child then listens to its own incarnating process through the ether body. It is a child of the cosmos from birth to seven, and it acts out what the pattern of stimulus-response would be in the particular organ that is secreting. That, in the language of anthroposophy and in pedagogy, is called fantasy.

The fantasy life of the child is driven by the sensations that are impacting the ether body, this earthly ether body that is creating secretions as images out of the cosmic formative patterns. So if there is acting out, the teacher looks to the environment and tries to create—especially for the liver—a kind of rhythmical massage of the liver. Day after day, things are presented and then moved on bit by bit, always building in a rhythmical way, and allowing for very clear pictures to go into sleep. The clearer the picture,

the more the liver can get it. The liver has a very dull consciousness. It is not tremendously aware of itself, we could say, but it is very much aware of what is coming to it. Three quarters of your liver can be removed, and it will regenerate. That is tremendous life. The characteristic of life is that it grows and decays, but it is not terribly aware. So during the birth-to-seven period, there is tremendous life pouring in through the senses of the young child. Fantasy arises in the child as a response to these sensations. The educator who looks at the environment and the rhythm of sensation has the best handle on being able to heal those liver rhythms of waking and sleeping and dreaming day-to-day.

When this happens in the environment of the child, there will not be a hunger for images when he is thirty-five. He won't succumb to the great temptation of striving to out-do the next person by inundating himself with sensations. The great struggle of adults today is to somehow transform their sensing.

This lecture was given February 21, 2000 as part of a series. It is printed here with the kind permission of Rudolf Steiner College Press who publishes the series under the title Knowledge, Teaching and the Death of the Mysteries. *Dennis Klocek is the director of the Goethean Studies Program at Rudolf Steiner College in Fair Oaks, California. He has written many articles and books, including* Seeking Spirit Vision.

Birth, Infancy
and the
First Years of Life

Child Development—Conception to Birth Embryology from an Anthroposophical Perspective

Bruno Callegaro, M.D.
Translated by Nina Kuettel

From the Waldorf Journal Project #2

Embryology is a modern science. It was in the Renaissance that isolated researchers such as Leonardo da Vinci first showed a quickened interest in the subject. Two to three hundred years later, the evolution of thinking and fundamentally important research by Goethe, Olken, Carus, and others created the basis for the study of embryology and the idea of metamorphosis associated with it. Systematic research in embryology was only well established after 1940.

This new scientific possibility offered the public the ability to actively engage their thoughts on the interval where invisible transformation takes place between two visible phenomena, since only isolated phenomena can be found during pregnancy examinations or after miscarriages. Continuous development as it is described in textbooks cannot be directly observed.

All that we see are microscopic "snap-shots." This is the result of an activity—an invisible transformation, or metamorphosis—in the interval between two visible forms. Films that show this continuous development are attempts to make the transformation graphically clear. However, it always remains invisible and can only be comprehended through the activity of thought. It is just this activity of thought that is new. It has only been possible for about one hundred years, since the end of the nineteenth century.

It assumes the modern ability to transcend with consciousness the threshold between that which can be perceived by the senses and that which is extrasensory.

Reproduction is a process of biological life, like breathing, blood circulation, digestion, and so forth. Maturation of sperm cells and egg cells is a particular specialization of the reproduction process. Reproduction is constant. For instance, the skin constantly renews itself, intestinal mucous membrane, blood, and hair are always growing. Reproduction penetrates the entire organism at varying tempos: the intestinal mucous membrane renews itself every four days, the skin every four weeks, the blood every hundred days. The slowest substances are the nerves. They need about seven years in order to fully regenerate themselves.

Within this intensive renewal activity, there is one that is specific—the formation of gametes (mature male and female reproductive cells). This is the only place where an organism biologically divides itself into male and female. The gametes are formed within the genitals, in the gonads of ovaries or testicles. This intensive cellular fluid regeneration is the matter, indeed, the **content** of an organism.

The preservation of **form**, however, can be found in the invisible archetypes. They come out

25

of the astral body and are active in the life body, lead by the individuality, the "I." The appearance of form is forever maintained through constitutive archetypes that hide themselves from sensual perception.

The cells of a human body are not isolated but rather found in tissue, enmeshed in fluid, strands, and filaments. The human body is 75–95% liquid, depending upon age and organ. Human tissue is tender and weak in its structure since it has comparatively little firm material contained within a lot of fluid. In tissue, substances are constantly transforming themselves. Confined by the skin, every cell is an organized collection of matter within liquid. It is like a living drop that breathes, extends, and then concentrates itself. There is a moment of maximum extension (with the thinning of the fluid) and a moment of maximum concentration (with the thickening of the fluid). A cell pulses between the thinned, extended state and the thick, viscous, concentrated state. Chromosomes can only be observed as protein strands in the thicker phase, and at that time take on a characteristic form. As cells, they continue to pulsate, extending, thickening, and then the chromosomes dissolve. This dissolution is equal to the cell becoming chaos. It opens itself to the potency of formative forces in that it loses its earlier form in order to create itself anew. That is how the form is kept alive and the re-forming of cells and tissue is ensured, depending upon the situation and need.

Chromosomes, like other cellular structures, are the results of condensation of formative archetypes in matter and not causes of form characteristics. The word chromosome means "a colored strand"—they are the structures that lend themselves the most to coloration when preparing cells for examination under a microscope. Genes are the conceptual parts of chromosomes that are arbitrarily apportioned along the length of these strands. The name comes from the word *genesis* and means "divine creation." The Creator wants to be found in the smallest biological structure. Cell division (mitosis) is an important process of reproduction. Cells divide themselves through mitosis at differing rates. Meiosis is the special form of cell division in the gonads, a specialized exception found nowhere else.

In the process of mitosis, the cell doubles itself and divides in such a way that two new cells come about that quantitatively resemble each other. In the process of meiosis there are two phases: the first is a mitosis and the second is a division without a previous doubling. The end result is that from one starting cell, four are created which, however, contain each only half the genetic material. This process pertains to the formation of sperm cells in the testicles. With the formation and maturation of egg cells in the ovaries, only one egg cell is produced from every ancestral cell, and not four, because the others dissolve themselves as polar bodies during the process. After maturation, the gametes are excreted by means of sperm ejaculation or menstrual bleeding, and they die. Only when impregnation takes place can an egg cell and a sperm cell, as a fertilized egg cell, live on in a new way and in a new form. Gametes themselves are not fertile. They expire after their long and complicated maturation if impregnation has not taken place. However, simultaneous with fertilization they reach a new qualitative level of life, without dying. They serve as a development basis for the formation of a new organism that is biologically and materially different from the mother-organism, wherein the egg cell was formed, and from the father-organism, where the sperm cell was formed.

Differentiation that occurs in the genetic stream and the gametes (reproductive cells):

Just as gametes, after their long maturation, leave the organism and perish as infertile and biologically unfit cells, other differentiating qualities can be determined. What are their differentiating qualities and role in the reproductive process?

Let us begin with the egg cell. Already in the fourth week of pregnancy, within the embryo, there begins the organic construction of what will later become the new child's reproductive organs and the first cells that will develop further into sex cells. This construction is, at first, common to both sexes and is still undifferentiated. After the fourth week of pregnancy, if the embryo develops further into a female organism, this biological composition develops one-sidedly towards the inside, back, and upward and loses the other spatial directions. However, the right-to-left symmetry remains. Then the ovaries develop as well as the uterus, the fallopian tubes, and the vagina. The long maturation of the egg cells is already initiated in the ovaries in the fourth week of pregnancy but they will rest between the first and second phase of meiosis until puberty. The rhythmic ovulation process begins at puberty when month to month one "egg cell" is released from an ovary: one time from the right, one time from the left. During the hours of ovulation, a localized rise in temperature occurs around the ovary. A mature egg cell is one of the largest cells in the human body; measuring approximately 0.1 millimeters, it is within the realm of visibility. This cell is still not a mature egg cell because the second phase of meiosis is completed only during an eventual impregnation. If no impregnation takes place, this immature cell dies and is expelled from a woman's body during menstruation, along with the spent uterine lining.

The egg cell is a turbid cell without its own power of movement. It rests within the surrounding follicle and is moved into the uterus by the peristaltic action of the fallopian tube. This follows after two weeks of building up in the time between the last menstruation and ovulation. Then there is another two weeks of building up between ovulation and the next menstruation. The egg cell becomes chaotic through its differentiation and its comprehensive range of chemical potential. In this state of chaos, it is especially sensitive and open to cosmic archetypes. From the fourth week of pregnancy, the male development also begins in the common organic construction during which phase the male gametes, the sperm or spermatozoa, are developed. The male organs develop towards the outside, the front, and downward. The right-to-left symmetry remains.

Maturation of the sperm is also at rest until puberty. However, after puberty, sperm formation is not rhythmic or regular, and with every ejaculation—which can occur many times a day and is influenced by sensual stimulation—thousands of mature sperm are ejected and perish. The reduced temperature of the testicles, which are outside the body, is critical to male fertility. Sperm cells are one of the smallest cells in the human organism.

Sperm is highly differentiated and thoroughly formed. It has a crystalline structure and, because of its high degree of crystallization, almost no chemical potential. Sperm are transparent cells with their own power of movement (disorganized, directionless, and fast). These are earthly qualities. So, it is clear that with the separation of the sexes, a kind of onesidedness appears, an extreme polarization between the male and female reproductive cells. At the end of the process, every gamete is biologically unviable and perishes. The following table shows a comparison of the polarization:

Female	Male
One	Thousands
Slow to mature	Quick to mature
Large	Tiny
Regularity	Irregularity
Rhythmic	Arrhythmic
Chaos	Form
Inside	Outside
Back	Front
Up	Down
Warm	Cold
Clouded	Transparent
Unmoving, inert	Power of movement
Chemical potential	Crystallized

The fertilization process is first initiated by a localized rise in temperature during ovulation. Once a month, between the last and next menstruation, in the middle of the menstrual cycle, a rhythmic temperature rise occurs in the mother-organism. Within this warmth of ovulation, an egg cell is released along with its surrounding follicle. The last phase of egg cell maturation begins outside of the ovary. The released egg cell is received by one of the fallopian tubes and is moved further along towards the uterus by its peristaltic action.

The egg cell is cooled somewhat in this process. Spermatozoa in the semen come toward the egg cell. Their path goes from the vagina in the direction of the uterus. Sperm come from the outside, from a cooler temperature, and warm themselves along the way. That is the first step of fertilization and takes place before the two cells come into contact with each other. The undifferentiated, warm, chaotic state of the egg cell is differentiated and cooled by the sperm. Within the meeting of these two genetic streams, a warmth organism is formed. The polarities of one-sided and extreme cold

and warmth are overcome. The individuality, the ("I") form the warmth organism from the balance that has occurred. The next step is the meeting of the gametes or reproductive cells. The egg cell is surrounded by thousands of sperm and in this moment a rhythmic rotation begins that lasts approximately thirty-six hours. A biochemical glow begins. There is still no penetration by a spermatozoon, but a light-organism has formed accompanied by ordered and harmonious movement. This is the second step of fertilization. Now, the individuality of the child has overcome the cloudy and inert state of the egg cell and the transparent, self-powered disordered-movement state of the spermatozoa and has again developed a light/movement organism out of the balance. The third step is what is traditionally known as actual fertilization, but is, in fact, the third process. A spermatozoon penetrates the egg cell, and its outer membrane chemically isolates itself from the mother-organism:

The first immunity processes begin. The other sperms die and dissolve. The egg cell goes through its last maturing by a process of further undifferentiating and chaos and by secretion of the so-called polar body, a concentrate of hardened cell material that is incapable of life. A rejuvenation of the egg cell occurs in this moment of intense activity between the egg cell and the differentiating determinations of the spermatozoon. The spermatozoon loses its crystalline structure, swells up, expands, and then dissolves in the plasma of the impregnated cell. An egg has now been formed—a biological and genetically complete cell. This cell then divides for the first time (mitosis), and other divisions rhythmically follow. There is not yet any growth, merely cell divisions in geometric progression—one becomes two, then four, eight, sixteen, thirty-two, and so on. The morula is formed while still inside the fallopian tube (like a little mulberry or raspberry). This organism does not glow and has no power of movement itself. The entire activity is now

28

chemical-biological and has relocated to the inner, light organism. The organism has overcome the polarities of potential chaos. A crystal forms and builds a chemical organism out of the balance, a new deed of the individuality.

The fourth step of fertilization is implantation into the mucous membrane of the uterus that has built up in the two weeks after menstruation and reached a high point in its development around the time of ovulation. Without fertilization (and the beginning of pregnancy), the mucous membrane would again deteriorate, and the dead tissue would be expelled with the next menstruation. With the implantation, which is an activity of the child, the built-up state of the mucous membrane and the hormone situation maintains itself until birth. The morula is still inside the fallopian tube (right or left) and then goes out so that it can fall into the uterus between the fifth and seventh days after conception. During this first experience with "falling" (weight, heaviness), the morula reshapes itself into a blastula or blastocyst. Here we have an organism that on one pole has formed a bladder filled with intercellular fluid, while on the other pole the cells of the no-longer-existing morula are thickened. During the process of falling, a polarization appears between cell thickness and fluid lightness. This changes the form of the organism. If the blastocyst was not an individualized, living totality, but rather an inorganic sphere, it would either burst in the mucous membrane or spring back into uterine space. However, it is embedded in the wall of the uterus—rather like an act of acceptance or receiving. The organism is now going through a new metamorphosis, and there is a recoil as the inner activity of the organism stays within itself, and there is a falling into heaviness but with a balancing buoyancy. A new fluid has formed at the pole where the cells were bunched. It is transparent, rich in silica, and poor in organic material, the amniotic fluid. The fluid that formed during the descent of the blastocyst is thicker, chemically active, and rich in material, the yolk sack fluid. In between is found the embryonic disk from which the body of the embryo will be formed. These two fluids are the first two enveloping organs of the embryo. In this fourth deed of the individuality, the separation of space that is typical for the female as well as the male sexual organs was overcome. With implantation a geographic location is chosen. A physical organism is formed that takes part in the laws of weight and lightness and the dimensions of space.

Fertilization, accompanied by the four deeds of the individuality that create balance, has overcome the extremely one-sided tendency to dissimilarity and separation of the sexes, and within one week and four steps has formed an individual organism that carries immunity, an organism that is four-fold in that it has the qualities of warmth, light, movement, and is biologically/chemically and physically/geographically localized. Implantation, the last step of fertilization, is simultaneously the first phase of formation of the amnion. Fertilization and the organic forms that follow are already the visible results of contention between the genetic material and the individual constitution of the incarnating child. The localized rise in temperature during ovulation of the mother-organism is the first accommodating, genetic, organic activity that is encountered by the individual, the child who wishes to incarnate. It builds a bridge out of the earthly genetic stream to the individuality and its constitution, which was already prepared before conception.

The individual constitution prepares itself in a world that is inaccessible to sense observation, the world that is in the interval between visible forms. A kernel of enthusiasm from the sea of will is what inflames the individual motive to incarnate and begin a new life. This "midnight world" before conception is the highest experience of spiritual development until after death. It is an awareness of the goals of human development in the present time and a growing enthusiastic absorption for the task of realizing those goals within their karmic webs on earth. This enthusiasm for the realization of the human acts like a magnet and draws the will toward the solicitous interest of all the spiritual hierarchies. A body of differentiated starlight—a star-body or astral body—envelops this kernel of spiritual enthusiasm. The will of the hierarchies to take part, with their presence, in the human creation of individuals is so great that the universe is threatened with becoming empty. But thanks to the cosmic reproduction force of healing and re-generation, the effects of the stars remain as en-velopment around the kernel of individuality and the beings themselves remain sustained in the universe. A new body, a new covering, whether cosmic or etheric, now also belongs to the indi-vidual constitution. Each individual "I" forms itself out of certain characteristics of its own, and this composition differentiates it from others that are likewise formed out of the same compo-nents and properties but in different configura-tions. This is the spiritual physical body—one's own physical body within its spiritual being. It cannot yet be perceived by the senses because it is not yet penetrated by matter.

This four-fold individual constitution has occasioned the meeting between father and mother out of a line of ancestors, and, from the time of fertilization, it will begin to penetrate the genetic stream, fusing, overcoming, and transforming the organism so that it becomes a tool for its own destiny. Enthusiasm for the development of humankind joins itself to the warmth as an organic agent; indeed, it is the warmth in the organic. The hierarchical will-archetypes work in light and in ordered move-ment. The chemical activity of the cells and cell divisions is subordinate to these archetypes that imprint them into matter, and, through this organic connection, matter is transformed over time. The individual destiny that wants to fashion itself takes on a form in this way and allows traces of its acts upon the earth into the dimensions of space.

The formation of the embryonic amnion began with the last step of fertilization—the implantation. The embryonic disk, a two-lay-ered cellular disk in the middle of the sphere that embedded itself into the uterine mucous membrane, will rest another two weeks during the formation of the amnion. The yolk sack is a thick, cloudy, chemically active organ. It is con-fined through one of the two embryonic disks called the endoderm or inner skin. Its functions are nutrition and metabolism.

The amnion is a transparent, vitreous organ. Equipped with light and formative forces, it is chemically inactive. It is, in turn, confined by the other layer of the embryonic disk, the ectoderm or outer skin. The allantois (sausage-like) is another amnion organ, out of the yolk sack and differentiated as a protuberance with the func-tions of elimination and detoxification. The entire outer spherical surface that is in direct contact with the uterine mucous membrane, along with the mother-organism, constitutes the fourth amnion organ.

Later the chorion further develops into the placenta. This organ intermediates between the two organisms, the mother and the fetal child. Within the mother-organism, the heredity—the past—resides, for the time of the pregnancy; this is the four-fold present organism of the child. This organism in turn carries or surrounds in its interior a third organism that will become the organism for the future. During the pregnancy, it will be elaborated upon by the individuality of the child for the time after birth. The four enveloping organs (embryonic amnions) fashion a complete organism with these four systematic functions:

a) Nutrition, metabolism Yolk Sack

b) Transparency, form Amnion

c) Elimination, detoxification Allantois

d) Exchange with environment, circulation Placenta (Chorion)

The motor system, the limb system, is still missing from this organism. It is present in the embryo body, but it will first develop and mature after the birth in contention with the earthly forces. In the middle, between these four enveloping organs, is the embryonic disk that rests until the seventeenth day after conception.

In the first week, fertilization is completed. It is finalized with implantation, the step that includes formation of the enveloping organs. By the end of the third week, the organism has been formed in which the individuality will live until birth (amnions). The embryonic disk is in the middle of this organism. From the seventeenth day until the end of the fourth week, the individuality molds the organism surrounding the embryonic disk until it is efficiently reorganized into an embryonic body.

This body contains all the organs that will serve as tools for the individuality after birth. By the end of the first month, the individuality has already built up its own organism in one shot. The individuality exists not only in relationship to space, but also to time—the 36-hour rotation and glow in the second step of fertilization, the day of implantation, and so forth. Every month of pregnancy has its own underlying characteristic. During pregnancy, the child experiences the course of the year for the first time. Birth comes at the end of the third quarter of this first year. The first three months after birth also belong to pregnancy because the individuality must contend with earthly conditions for the first time and ripens its physiology based upon what is living in its environment.

The development of the embryonic organs from the amnions begins on the seventeenth day after conception. Until then the embryonic disk is resting and the creation activity is in the amnions. The embryonic disk consists initially of two skins, the ectoderm and the endoderm, which confine the yolk sack and the amnion sack.

The first noticeable gesture of the reshaping of the embryonic disk occurs on the ectoderm around the seventeenth day. At the place where the head pole will develop, an impression appears, as if an invisible finger had imprinted it. Out of this the neural cavity develops away from the head pole. This indentation as well as the neural cavity determines the anatomic spatial bearing—right, left, i.e. the lateral symmetry, caudal, dorsal, and ventral. The neural cavity develops further into the neural tube, thereby closing in amnion fluid that, from this point in time, will surround the nerve system as cerebrospinal fluid. The first rudiments of the spinal cord and the vertebrae have appeared. Later on, the back is reminiscent of the ectoderm of the embryonic disk. The sensitive area around the fourth thoracic vertebra is a memory of the area around that first impression. The disk form reshapes itself into an oblong showing the tendency to form like the neural tube. An intermediate skin, the mesoderm, is formed between the ectoderm and the endoderm. Now the rounding formation tendency of the endoderm and the yolk sack becomes spherical and is internalized in the body.

There are two polar formation tendencies clearly displayed. Chronologically, the first is the formation of the skin and the nerve-sense system from the ectoderm and runs linear, oblong, and towards the outside. The last formation chronologically builds the structure of the digestive and metabolic systems from the endoderm and runs spherical, round, and towards the inside. In the middle chronologically, between the linear and the round tendencies, the rhythmic waves of the mesoderm are acting, mediating between the facing polar tendencies. Finally, the round tendency will form the typical round, circular shape of the embryonic countenance. Likewise, from the endoderm a tube develops, although internalized—the structure of the digestive tract from the mouth to the anus with all the organs that belong to it. The content of this digestive tube is the yolk fluid, and the embryo is completely surrounded by amniotic fluid. Connective tissue, the muscles and cartilage, is formed from the mesoderm. On one side, this connective tissue fills the space between the nerve-system, the sense-organs, and the skin and, on the other side, that of the metabolic-digestive systems. The chorion is the outermost sphere of the embryonic amnions and develops into the placenta. Here, outside the embryonic body, blood formation begins. Islands of blood flow into the yolk fluid and penetrate the body. They favor certain stream paths that are enclosed by the mesoderm and formed into blood vessels. Two main vessels, at first outside of the body, are formed at the heart, in front of what will be the ribcage, and the throat directly underneath the developing head. However, before the ribcage completely closes, the heart penetrates and fills it.

The urinary bladder and the sexual organs are formed from the allantois together with the endoderm and the yolk sack. Formation of the kidneys, however, comes out of the nerve system—their beginning structure is located in the back of the brain. This structure develops from the brain immediately under the skin in two rows of little "pearls" along the spinal cord further to the dorsal area. The "pearls" close to the head degenerate and those at the dorsal area wrap themselves, taking on the spherical without losing their lateral symmetry. Here a neural tendency is brought into the vicinity of the metabolic system.

The lungs are formed from a protuberance of the digestive tract. By dividing in half the lungs are placed in a three-fold symmetry to the branching of the bronchia and the alveolar system inside the ribcage—right to left, cephal and caudal, front to back. Here a metabolic tendency is brought into the vicinity of the nerve system.

Simultaneously with lung formation, hand formation begins immediately followed by the feet, then the lower arms and calves, and finally the upper arms and thighs. The lungs are formed together with the limbs. After the birth, they serve together in the life on earth and in the air. By the end of the fourth week, all the structures of the embryonic organs are formed. This process was completed in about ten days. In the prior three weeks, fertilization, implantation, and formation of the enveloping organs were completed.

Birth usually happens at the end of the third quarter. The fourth quarter is the first three months of life outside of the mother-organism. Now important maturing processes and restructuring of the organs take place. These processes require contact with gravity and the atmosphere outside the womb, but are still considered processes belonging to pregnancy. It is important to get to know the characteristic of each of the twelve months.

- The first month brings the summary of all the components of the enveloping organs and the body. Out of the gaze toward the past, it is an all-embracing acceptance of the universe and the first assimilation of wholeness. With the help of Rudolf Steiner's indications for eurythmy, the formative gesture of **Aries** can be recognized.

- The second month shows the assimilation of the mobility of the universe, the first inner movements, the beginning physiology. The "gaze" turns to the present and future, the universe now in this life, the formative gesture of **Taurus**.

- In the third month, the individuality begins to experience the body. The first tactile experiences follow. The hands and feet touch each other, the two sides touch each other, the formative gesture of **Gemini**.

- In the fourth month, the body's immunity and resistance are so far structured and developed that the formative gesture of **Cancer** can be recognized, to close oneself off from the environment. These first four months have, as their priority, formation out of the universe, starting from the head.

- In the fifth month, the inner regions of the

organism have been filled, the ribcage developed, the gesture of **Leo**.

- In the sixth month, important maturing processes take place. From this month onward, the body exhibits more and more organic resistance in order to survive a possible premature birth, the gesture of **Virgo**.

- The seventh month brings new contentions with weight and heaviness for the pregnant woman. The child practices balance and placement, the gesture of **Libra**.

- The eighth month can bring with it the danger of reciprocal poisoning, the first contention with earthly matter, the nearness of death around the time of birth, the gesture of **Scorpio**. These middle four months address themselves to inner-formation—the torso.

- The nearness of the birth also brings with it the contention with the earth, with the will that is served by the limbs, with breathing, with the gradual introduction of nutrition and with digestion, with learning of sleep and changing states of consciousness, with the maturing of the warmth organism. These processes ripen after birth with the formative gestures of

Sagittarius, Capricorn, Aquarius, and Pisces.

The last months of pregnancy and likewise the first months of life address themselves to the first calisthenics of the limbs and the metabolism in conjunction with earth forces. These characteristics of the twelve months of the year can serve as an orientation and help us get to know the psychological mood of the mother and child during pregnancy. The organic contributions of the mother to the birth are the rhythmic muscle contractions, the intensity and characteristics of which change around the time of the birth.

Normally the *first phase* of the birth appears with the placement of the child's head at the opening to the birth canal from the cervix going in the direction of the vagina. It is the expression of the child's will to set his/ herself in contention with the earth. Again, the head pole, the nerve system, is the first. The individuality of the child, which is still living in the enveloping organs, begins to leave them in order to move into the organs of the body. The first step is the death of the amnion fluid when the amniotic sack breaks. The nerve-sense activity now begins to move into the head. The head searches for the way outside and, as a result, the child's forehead comes in contact with the mother's pelvic bone.

At this moment, the child is in complete solitude and cannot be helped from the outside. The child must find the so-called hypomochlion, that is a search for balance between life in the womb, its past, and turning to the earth, its goal and future. Hypomochlion is also the name of the balancing point on a scale. At the moment of birth, the gesture of the child's head is an exaggerated downward position of the chin in order to free the forehead so that the head can go upward: this is the first gesture of erectness and verticality. The light of the world will be seen. After this first obstacle is overcome, the body is born, usually head first. Later, it will always be the limbs that carry out the will and lead movement. After birth, the head attains a state of rest, places itself at the top, in lightness. The child is taken into the mother's arms. In the *second phase*, the child begins to breathe and experiences a string of changes and maturations in the cardiovascular system. It begins to draw upon the middle system of the new body. The umbilical cord now stops pulsing, the placenta dies and is expelled. Hours after birth when the child has been diapered, has maybe already slept, the excretion of the meconium occurs. This is not yet a stool, but rather the demise of the yolk fluid contained in the intestine. In the *third phase* of birth, the child has now begun to draw upon the digestive and metabolic system.

With the first urination, one has the outer sign that the child, in a *fourth phase*, has stirred the organs of excretion and detoxification. The allantois now dies. The dead allantois remains as a holdover in the organism as a fatty strand, the *ligamentum paraumbilicale*. Birth has four phases just like fertilization. The individuality gradually grasps the four functional main systems. Birth is accompanied by the deaths of the four enveloping organs that will be left behind. Birth has a *past* (excretion of the amnion fluid, head movement, and maturation of the nerve system), a *present* (the first breath, changes in the heart and circulation, and the death of the placenta), and a *future* (excretion of the meconium and the metabolic system beginning to mature—which will not be finished in a lifetime). And, as a remembrance of mortality, a "poisonous sting," the *ligamentum paraumbilicale* remains in the organism after birth.

The individuality no longer has a spherical organism in its surroundings. It now begins to have its own organism as its center that step by step is grasped and penetrated for at the least the next eighteen to twenty-one years. It is the task of adults to form and act as the new enveloping organs, to support the individuality within the surroundings of its own body, and to help with the efforts to individualize the newborn organism. There will still be many different births of the individuality and many deaths of what was inherited in the further course of development that should, from now on, be educationally and pedagogically accompanied.

೦ೖ

Dr. Bruno Callegaro has practiced anthroposophical medicine in South America and in Germany where he is a faculty member of the Rudolf Steiner Institute in Kassel. He has participated in courses and conferences throughout the English-speaking world, lecturing on child development.

Making Sense of Uprightness

Bonnie and William RiverBento

When we understand incarnation as an ongoing process of childhood rather than merely as a physical event at birth, we extend our responsibility as adults beyond parenthood. All the early childhood caregivers and teachers become involved in the child's incarnation. This fact complicates the incarnation process, but also provides hidden resources and opportunities for the child. Our modern day challenge is to educate ourselves to a process that, in times of old was a natural unfolding, but which is under attack today from many directions.

In the first few months of life the infant is completely dependent upon others for its mobility in space. Although the hands and feet are capable of movement, they do not have sufficient strength to move the torso any measurable distance. This dependency wanes in the third and fourth months and the infant "plays" into moving her own body through a steady progression of movements, which culminate in crawling and exploring the world around her.

The child, while lying on her back in the horizontal plane, extends her hands above her, and they wave and reach upward, becoming perpendicular to the body. The limbs lead the child toward uprightness. If the child is allowed sufficient time on her back, she will develop the torso muscles needed for stability in the upright position and will be able to bear her own weight.

The whole process of turning oneself over to face the earth and then coming to the upright on earth is a vital step in ego development. Through these intricate movements, the child comes to touch the self and to touch the earth in right relationship. Stability of torso, stability in the soul, and stability in the vessel which receives the essential and unique human being, these are the gifts of these first movements through the dimensions of space. Uprightness is a miraculous achievement for the child, yet it is also the beginning of a new set of challenges. The geography of the body and orientation to space needs to be learned. The acquisition of these skills involves a delicate interplay between the body in movement and the senses.

The sense of well being, which is an organic sense of life functions, helps to establish a healthy relationship to the earthly planes. In and through the head the outer world enters through the portals of the senses. The head is the highest part of our organism, and the air we breathe, the light we receive, and the food we eat can all be seen as nourishment, which enters from above and descends down into the body. When this is functioning healthily, the nutrients give to the limbs the power to move in space.

Watch the little child toddle through space to grasp hold of something in the world around him. In his ego-being he seeks to grasp the world, to begin his own digestion of the world around him. When we examine digestive processes from a phenomenological viewpoint, we cannot help but marvel at the journey of all that is to be digested. In eating, the food must be lifted, moved horizontally, tumbled through all the planes as we chew, and then it descends. Follow it through the interior spaces. It goes on a similar journey to that of objects that come into the grasp of the toddler.

Now imagine a child grasping a fake plastic rock. It looks like granite, has the appearance of being heavy, yet as he grasps it, his hand flies into the air, for every fiber of his body was prepared for the weight! He is shocked and learns not to trust his senses. Can we draw an analogy to the body and digestion? Does the body know when it is being fooled? Is food that is chemically altered grasped as truthful by the digestion? During this time of childhood, trust in the truthfulness of the world around and within is gained. The concept of "rock" is true when the child touches it, and he is secure in his thinking about the forces of earth. A sense of security in conceptual ability is based in healthy digestion.

Now let us watch the toddler as she moves into the world around her. Her rocking and shuffling movements gradually articulate into the cross lateral and balanced weight shifting movements of human walking. Through rocking back and forth, the weight and balance is shifted over the saggital midline. The child experiences left and right and gradually the center, from which the limbs will move freely. This outer movement is reflected in human statements such as, "On one hand, I see it this way, while on the other, it is thus." These statements reveal a higher nature to thinking of concepts. Through a healthy development of movement, the child develops the language of clear articulation of concepts.

As the child's walk becomes refined, the child gains a sense of mastery in his balance. The sense of balance is not a static phenomenon but a dynamic one, which mature in the child when

a genuine ability to come to a state of rest is achieved. This sense is deeply connected to the frontal plane; both front and backspaces are involved. Although most of our senses are oriented to the front space, we also have a mysterious backspace. Without it we could easily be drawn into every sense impression that meets us from the world; in the backspace we have a counterweight to this pull into the world around us. We can in both a physical and a metaphoric sense turn our back to the world and listen to our own response to it.

Consider the agitated, restless child, who moves incessantly and finds no peace in inward "listening." These children, growing in number, and often labeled as having an attention related disorder, are revealing a disturbing psychological profile. They tend to exhibit mistrust of the world around them, a lack of true autonomy, and an inability to sustain initiative in a task that is not of strictly personal interest.

In Bonnie's work with Attention Related Disorders studies, she very often finds that these children have a history of early childhood ear infections. These are accompanied by rounds of antibiotics and all sorts of interventions such as tubes in the ears. These children have experienced a very real disturbance in their ability to come to true balance and in their ability to learn to listen. When we journey past the middle ear and into the inner ear, we see two wondrous "organs," the vestibular apparatus and the cochlear formation, joined together at the "vestibule" by the major exiting cranial nerve, the vestibular nerve. The impulses, which travel down this nerve, serve to inform us regarding the sound we hear and the space we occupy. In a concerted way, they serve to establish the human ability to maintain balance and hearing. Thus we see that balance and hearing work together intimately. In order not to just "fall into" something, we need to listen and discriminate well.

To protect and guide the great deeds the child must accomplish—those of coming to uprightness, grasping the world and coming to restful listening—we need to gird ourselves with a deep understanding of these forces. With such understanding, we protect children from the very forces that threaten to rob them of these incarnating rites of passage. Consider the forces that tug at parents to place their child into an apparatus that will "give" the child an upright experience and that inhibits the ability to grasp the world and dampens the child's sense of peace and listening. This powerful tug must be met with a joyful, loving knowing of the child's bill of rights, which could begin with, "Every child is endowed with the right to playfully and freely explore being in a body and in the space around him; and through an experience of truth in his surroundings, he will come to trust the world and sense his holy and autonomous self, living in a temple of stability and restful listening."

&

William RiverBento has been an avid student and practitioner within the field of human development for over thirty years. He is currently enrolled in a doctoral program at the Institute of Transpersonal Psychology in Palo Alto, CA. His special interest is star wisdom.

Bonnie RiverBento has been a Waldorf early childhood educator, class teacher and educational support teacher at a number of Waldorf schools and teaches courses in remedial/therapeutic education. She and William are co-founders of Gradalis Seminars, and are active consultants in Waldorf and therapeutic communities internationally.

The Wonder of Acquiring Speech

Michaela Glöckler, MD

What do walking, talking and thinking have in common? They are not encoded into us in a fixed manner as some things that are genetically determined. Rather, they arise from within the child through the process of imitation. These capabilities can develop only if certain activities happen which involve the child.

An example was given of a thirteen-year-old girl who, out of criminal neglect, never learned to speak. She was kept in an imprisoned state and grew up mute. Then she was discovered at age thirteen, and her overall intelligence was less than that of a two-year-old. In the next two years, she learned a great deal. She developed speech, but it was an unusual form of speech. If she wanted to say, "I don't like the color on the walls," she would express it by saying, "No—wall color." Her speech developed in two word sentences. She was right-handed, but her speech center was on the right side, rather than the left. This is quite unusual, for in 97% of people, the speech center, known as the Broca center, is on the left side of the brain. Normally the child learns to use this speech center through imitation, but this child was no longer sensitive to the development of the center through imitation. Instead, language developed in another part of the brain, on the right side, and it could not fully develop there. She developed language in the way that a very young child develops it—every-

thing is nice or not nice, yes or no. This thirteen-year-old spoke in this same way, beginning a sentence with "yes" or "no" and then giving a simple identification of what she liked or didn't like.

Different aspects of speech develop in different parts of the brain. For example, the first language, the mother tongue, develops in one part of the brain, but subsequent languages develop in another part. An example was given of a woman who had learned a German dialect as her mother tongue. Later she learned to speak "high German." After an accident that affected the brain, she lost her use of the high German, but her use of dialect remained, for that part of the brain had not been injured. In other cases of brain injury, one might be able to understand language, but not be able to speak it.

There is a strong element of wonder that arises when we consider speech and its development. Acquiring speech is not an inherited process but a process of learning. What are the preconditions for a child to learn speech? This is a complicated question, for there are many fundamental elements of speech, all of which need to develop. Consonants and vowels, for instance, have different qualities. The vowel element expresses how we feel, while the consonants are more directly related to the outer sense world. Every syllable contains both elements, so that each syllable builds a bridge from self to the world.

Rudolf Steiner said that the astral body is the carrier of the feeling for speech, but also to speak and understand speech, we need the capacity for thought and the functioning of the ego. It is not a simple matter. Physical parts of the body are also necessary for the formation of speech. The timbre or quality of the speech is related to the air flowing through the larynx, which is a very complicated organ in its own right. It contains a great many small muscles, as many muscles as one finds in the rest of the body. The larynx is like a little person, a miniature of the whole human being in movement. At the physical level, one also needs to take into account the form of the mouth with its palate, teeth and tongue. One book recommended to help understand this picture is *Erziehung ist Kunst* by Wolfgang Schad. It has not yet been translated into English. When we look at the shape of the mouth, we realize how closely related it is to the capacity for speech. The ape cannot speak, for instance, for its mouth is not formed for speech. The ape's mouth juts forward as it develops, whereas the human mouth grows backwards as the second teeth and molars come in. The front of the mouth of a young child and of an adult are more or less the same in form.

Beginning with the second year of life, the child experiences a continual development of speech. All parts of the mouth contribute to the development of speech, and if one part is adversely affected, it can affect the form of the speech to a greater or lesser extent. Speech develops in the child while the mouth itself is developing. Approximately one fourth of kindergarten-aged children have speech difficulties, but most will outgrow them by themselves. By adolescence, only one to two percent of them will still have problems. In most children, the problems disappear by age five or six. Others will stop having problems with the change in teeth,

so that by age eight or nine, most will no longer have difficulty in speech.

Wolfgang Schad gives a picture of language differences on the African continent in contrast to China. In Africa, from Tunisia to Capetown, one finds about seven hundred different languages in use. This does not count dialects that are also abundant. In contrast, in the whole huge land of China, there is only one language present. Also, China has had a written language from its earliest times, whereas Africa did not initially develop a written language. In Africa, the spoken word has great importance. It is full of magic.

In China, the written language is of great importance, and the written language is the same throughout the country. About four thousand characters are used in the written language of Chinese newspapers. More characters exist, but at the newspaper level, four thousand suffice for expression. People all over China can read the same newspaper and understand it. Even though they may pronounce the characters differently, they read them and understand them in the same way. The Chinese language is based on pictures, and the characters have remained much the same over time. There has been diversity and change in the language, but there is enough continuity that texts that are thousands of years old can still be easily read. In the German language, in contrast, texts written in the old German of the Middle Ages can no longer be read except by scholars. Each continent has its own qualities of soul life, and these are reflected in its language development. In China, we see a land unified by language in which the old forms can continue to live into the present. Thinking and speaking are closely aligned in China, whereas, in Africa, speaking and movement are more closely aligned. On the African continent with its seven hundred languages, social relations are of great importance. The basic quality of love has developed strongly there, as well as the social feeling for others. All of this flows out of the astral body very strongly in Africa. It is part of the picture of Africa, whereas China has a contrasting picture.

In the development of the child, we see language unfolding in different ways during the various stages of the child's growth. Between ages seven and fourteen, children love to play with language. They make jokes and play with words. This is a time when language is extremely important. Rudolf Steiner gave many indications about language to the class teachers. Dr. Glöckler feels that about seventy percent of discipline problems in the elementary grades can be met through more awareness of language. In contrast, about 70% of kindergarten discipline problems can be met through greater awareness of movement. It is so important that we speak well to the children. We should "clean" our speech organ like we clean our teeth each morning so that we can speak rightly to the children of different ages.

The teenager experiences a different aspect of language. They are looking for meaning, and sometimes feel meaning has gone. This can be a crisis for the individual. Eurythmy is of great help to them in finding meaning again in language. We must work to find sense in language in order to help the students. It is important for the children to meet an adult who speaks with an Ego consciousness. There are ways to work on language that help raise human speech to cosmic speech. For example, we can work on our relationship with the everyday words of the language and learn to love them, to set them free. The poor words that are used every day are no longer shining. We can love them and give them color. Then they laugh again.

Speech is our friend. If we feel depressed, we can take a poem, even a very simple one, and work it through word for word. We can speak the words in different ways, with strength or gentleness, for instance. We can hear how funny they sound when they are spoken with a quality not true to the word. It is difficult to capture and express inner qualities in words.

Speech lives very deeply within us and is related to our own I, or Ego. In paradise, Adam was asked to name all of the creatures. The memory of paradise lives on in our speech. Finding the self within is related to this process of giving names. Part of the mystery of the I is that it comes to birth and incarnation through a series of identifications. In early childhood, we identify with an activity such as dishwashing and take it into ourselves through imitation. In the elementary grades, we identify with the world in the soul realm through love. In adolescence, we identify at the thought level through interest. Through these three realms of interest, the I incarnates. Working through these realms, the I goes beyond physical nature and comes to discover its spiritual nature.

In the word, there is tremendous creative power that can be alive in us. The whole of world creation is in us and can be awakened more fully in us when we work on the word. The word became darkened through the fall of mankind, but we can bring new thinking and will to the realm of speech. It is our task as teachers to bring new qualities to speech so that a new consciousness can shine through. This is a great help to children as they seek to find their own Ego. If we reactivate the archetypal Adam within us, he who had the power to name things, then this newfound power of speech works creatively on the children.

Loving language should be today's motto.

Verse for the Beginning of Teaching
the Ancient Languages

Rudolf Steiner

To him who understands the sense of speech

To the spirit and soul of the world.

To him who hears the speech of the soul

The world reveals itself as a being.

He who experiences the speech of the spirit

Receives the world with the strength of wisdom.

He who is able to love speech

Is given its own power.

So I will turn to my heart and senses

And in love I will find myself

For the first time through it.

☙

Dr. Michaela Glöckler is currently the head of the Medical Section at the Goetheanum in Dornach, Switzerland. She has been active as a pediatrician and school doctor in Germany and is the author of A Guide to Child Health, *Floris Books.*

Movement, Gesture and Language in the Life of the Young Child

Bronja Zahlingen

We are filled with respect and wonder when we consider how each and every human individual, after coming from the spiritual world, is able to feel so at home with life on earth in the very earliest years. It is through the three important stages of becoming—walking, speaking and learning to think—that each child opens herself up to the conditions of her physical, soul and objective spiritual environment. It is like waves breaking on the shore, the constant interplay of the ebb and flow at the ocean's edge. The entire development of the earth is experienced again with the changing phases of metamorphosis.

After accomplishing these steps, the approximately three-year-old child can sense and name herself, "I." The human child, crown of creation, who raises herself above the realms of nature by means of these abilities, does so in order to work with, and to feel a loving attachment towards, these realms. The child learns to entrust herself to the earth's gravity and its substances, and she learns to overcome it actively through her own higher strengths if we kindly help out by offering our example and protection. Her stirring will wants to go in all directions. She wants to stand upright, to keep her balance between above and below and to walk. She wants to become one with the elements by running, jumping, hopping and sliding. She wants to turn and spin and dance around only to come to rest again and

again on good Mother Earth. Children have just such an experience in the old dance meant for the youngest ones:

> *Ring around the rosies*
> *A pocket full of posies.*
> *A tissue, a tissue*
> *We all fall down.*

Right away they do it again and again and again.

Children also love to run away—far away—until finally tired out, when they turn around and joyfully rush back into mother's protective arms. Or the child falls down. She would like to cry, but she stretches upwards again, like the little daisies in the meadow. After a heavy rain, the daisies are flattened, but with the first ray of sun, they raise their heads toward the light. Hence, the custom for English mothers to say, "Up a daisy" if their children trip or fall, and upon hearing it, each child stands gladly up again.

And then there is rocking, first gently in the cradle, half dreaming with soft songs, like being carried along the waves of life's water. Then this motion becomes stronger when they are riding on a knee:

This is the way the ladies ride,

Nimble, nimble, nimble, nimble;

This is the way the gentlemen ride,

A-gallop, a-trot, a-gallop, a-trot;

This is the way the farmers ride,

Jiggety-jog, jiggety-jog;

And when they come to a hedge—they jump over!

And when they come to a slippery place—

They scramble, scramble, scramble,

Tumble-down Dick!

When children are a bit older, the rocking motion is there in their swinging, which grows ever more courageous—up and down between heaven and earth. There are truly splendid, lively movements natural to children's games in which the ability to be upright and move rhythmically help to overcome the burden of gravity. "I am so heavy when I sit," said a young schoolboy, joining in an adult conversation about body weight. Children certainly can word their thoughts in such a precise and wonderful way.

The way each child moves—the solidity or inconsistency, the hesitancy or surety of her steps—reveal much about the nature of her will. Recognizing this, we can help to balance and harmonize the child. Once the child has attained the upright position and can keep her balance, her arms and hands become freer and can better grasp the world about her in various ways. This is truly unique to the human being, for the animal, still bound to its physical organization, must utilize its front limbs entirely to serve its body—they must carry and nourish it. We human beings can perform many different kinds of work. We can work with our hands as artists, we can wave and threaten, give and take, pray and bless.

With her arms and hands, the child thus gains a new area of expression—that of the self,

an inner, more soul-like quality of expression can be revealed in the "gesture." Archetypal gestures like expansion and contraction, opening and closing into width and narrowness, and tightening and loosening are fundamental gestures in life which are carried out either quickly or slowly, gently or powerfully. The true human gestures of work and all visible activities have been found in children's games as well as the gesture of things in their surroundings, which have taken on a permanent form. These are imitated as well in the soul and growth forces, thus having a strengthening or destructive effect.

Gesture precedes the development of language. Indeed, it goes hand in hand with the formation of the speech center in the brain. This also develops in correspondence with the use of the right or left hand. Such gestures as pushing, stooping, touching, grasping and letting go help to develop and form speech sounds. A fluctuation between opening and closing, tightening and loosening develops in conjunction with the rhythm of breathing, and this works on the shaping of the vocal chords and other speech organs. The teeth, lips, tongue, palate and larynx also have a part in this. The outer perception and the inner disposition delicately begin to be formed as soul gesture.

Now, in addition to crying, a child can tell us ever more clearly by the use of words and speech how she feels. When we deepen our study of Rudolf Steiner's rich and varied statements about human speech, its origin and effect, we also become more clearly aware that we unite ourselves with the spiritual in the world through our speech. When speech grows beyond the individual, physical-soul realm, it leads us into a greater more far-reaching realm, that of the formative creative word. Here we look with deepest gratitude to the essence of eurythmy and its inherent formative and healing power.

The mother tongue is as necessary and nourishing to a child's soul as mother's milk is to her body. The child gradually becomes accustomed to the sound and gesture of the language, its revelations in the rhythm and significance of the word. The meaning of a word is readily experienced by the child chiefly in a pictorial manner and not as abstract meaning and concept. For the child, it is the diverse, colorful and changing nature of life itself. She takes joy and refreshment in the language when it is abundantly and rhythmically expressed.

There are countless songs, verses and rhymes for children, both merry and serious, in everyday language and in more poetic form. These are a veritable horn of plenty at the disposal of parents and educators for moderate usage. Here are some examples:

Pick, pack, pull—will the pail soon be full?
Hinka, hanka, hat,
Where is the dog, where is the cat?
The dog is lying near the hearth
Giving himself a nice, clean bath.
The cat is sitting by the window
Licking her fur and each little toe.
Hinkety, pinkety, heckety, hairs,
The lady is coming up the stairs.
What is she bringing to the kitty?
A ball, a ball, a ball so pretty!
A woolly, white ball in the big house
That looks just like a little mouse.
And to her doggy what does she bring?
A handsome collar with a golden ring,
A handsome collar of a special kind
With doggy's name in front and behind.
Hinkety, pinkety, heckety, hout,
Now my tale is all told out.
—Christian Morgenstern

A fingerplay:

Ten little men, see, sitting under the tree.
The short and the fat are nodding like that.
The nimble and quick, they dance and they lick.
The long and the strong come running along.
The pretty ones sing for a golden ring.
The babies are tripping and laughing and skipping.
Be quiet you little ones, lie down and rest,
Tucked up in your cradle like birds in a nest.
—H. Diestel

An Old English verse:

Round about, round about
In a fair ring-a.
Thus we dance, thus we dance
And thus we sing-a
Trip and go, to and fro, over this green-a
All about, in and out
For our brave Queen-a

Or more reflective:

Song of the Sun

I am the Mother Sun and I carry the earth,
Through all the night and through the morning's birth.
I hold her safely and upon her do shine,
So that all that is living can grow up fine.
Human and animal, flower and stone
All share the light from me alone.
Open your heart like a little cup,
With my bright light I shall fill it up!
Open your heart, child so dear,
That we may become one light here.
—Christian Morgenstern

Nowadays we slip easily and quickly into the banal and even into the fantastic, which is devoid of any inner truth. Some examples of this are the comic strips, which offer children sheer absurdity. They even display what people say as mere air bubbles coming out of their mouths, and these often contain primitive noises (ugh, oof, et cetera).

Of course, the Word must at times descend from poetry to the level of prose, but it should at least be meaningful and serve Life. If it remains as mere information, the soul comes out empty-handed, without sympathy for others, in such a way that the social feeling and interest are not aroused.

One poet has already warned us:

"When the soul speaks so,

Then it is the soul no more."

—Schiller

Moreover, we print many words these days that only serve artificially as empty housing for advertising and profits. At the same time, the words and images of the best poets and painters are becoming distorted and strange, and they stare the passersby in the eye from every billboard and kiosk. Fortunately, sometimes a child is still naive and full enough of fantasy to come to his own conclusions, like the first grader who could already read a bit, and then asked at home, "Say, Mother, what is a naked wave anyway?" The mother was clearly in a big dilemma about how to answer him when her son solved the whole thing himself by saying, "Ah, I know—it is a wave without foam!"

Our thought life gradually grows into its various forms through the use of language and the formation of words and sentences. It leads step by step to abstraction and conceptualization, but this process is reserved for a later developmental stage (similar to how the whole development of language is accomplished.) Language need not become stiff or hardened, rather it will have to struggle through to new imaginations and higher levels. A conscious creative and artistic beginning will have to be found, as naivete is found in the creative, formative language of a child. The child, whose natural inclination is to have his own soul nature conform to that of the adult, needs gestures full of caring affection and helpfulness and a language full of truth. In the tone of the language, there also lies a gesture—one can caress with words, as well as explain and point out things. We can loosen what has become hardened and give it new, living form.

The immense impoverishment in the diminishing life forces of nature and the intellectualization of our whole cultural life threaten today's children. Our technical and automated civilization is far removed from the living nature of the small child. The media ruins her senses that need to develop firstly through active use and experience. Direct access to real life, to human gestures, to language and immediate experience of another individuality is falsified and destroyed by the media.

There are many children today who have been damaged in their entire ability to move, for they spend too much time sitting in the car, and they observe and imitate the mechanical running around that takes place on all sides. Thus they walk with stiff, automatic gestures, or they speed about imitating engine noises. There is no time or opportunity to pause, to catch sight of or overhear something more delicate and subtle. Today, we find so many basically intelligent, lovable, good-natured children who suddenly, without apparent cause, are seized by fidgeting, jerking and pushing, and who, at times, also seem to explode with strange noises.

Curative attention in movement, gesture and language will become ever more needed as we are able to gain a deeper, greater insight into the true nature of the human individuality in body, soul and spirit. New creative capabilities will

grow in us to replace our lost instincts as well.
It is only in this way that we can help to build
a suitably human future for and through the
children.

∾

Bronja Zahlingen was born in Austria; she studied early childhood education there until the outbreak of World War II, when she fled to England. There she taught in the Waldorf kindergarten at Michael Hall School before returning after the war to Vienna, where she helped found the Waldorf School. She had a special interest in the development of language and imagination in the young child and was known for her work with marionette plays, stories and verses, some of which are collected in Plays for Puppets, *published by WECAN.*

Supporting the Development of the Human Hand

Ingun Schneider

The hands of a musician gracefully flying across the piano keys, the fingers of a young student playing a recorder, or the hands of a sculptor molding clay into artistic forms—these are all situations which show the uniquely human quality of the hand. Observe the hands of a mother caressing her baby, an elderly couple holding hands, or a hand giving a friendly pat on a shoulder—the hands can freely offer solace, convey love, as well as give and receive gifts of service. Besides these heartfelt and creative pursuits, the human hand develops several practical capacities, mainly through the activities of childhood and youth. With precision and strength the hand can use a screwdriver, a saw, or a hammer; it can spin a top, sew on a button, paint a delicate picture, and write with a pen or pencil.

In today's push-button world the hand's marvelous capacity for skill has taken on a regimented and manipulative character rather than its birthright, a living, creative agility. Do the eyes lovingly follow what the hands are doing when the fingers are clicking away at a keyboard, moving a mouse, or pushing buttons on any other machine? This lack of connection between the eyes and the hands begins early these days as more and more young children stare at screens while their hands do nothing or move joysticks or push buttons in automatic ways. Does the rise in carpal tunnel syndrome and other ailments due to muscle tension in the neck, shoulders, and arms have anything to do with the ways we use our hands?

How our hands are used may not seem like an important issue in the education of the child, yet our human hands have a potential that no animal "hand" has[1]. The hands are the human being's most creative and selfless organs, in that our hands are free to offer service to others and to nourish and care for ourselves.[2] The development of the hand with its fine motor skills so necessary for managing the writing, drawing, and other artistic activities of school is an area often forgotten by today's parents and educators alike. Many teachers notice that children hold their pencils and crayons in awkward ways, but do not necessarily connect these tense pencil grips with the sensory and motor development of the hand and of the postural system.

The hand and arm are, of course, only a part of the whole. Yet the whole is present in the part. If we look at the hand we see the quiet center of the palm with the five delicate fingers raying out from it. The powerful heel of the palm can be seen as the will aspect of the hand, the center of the palm as the feeling aspect, and the fingers as the thinking part. The hand, arm, and shoulder are a trinity in themselves. The hand is related to the nerve-sense system, connected with thinking; the arm is the balancer in the center, related

49

to our feeling life, while the shoulder carries the will. The eye, in the meantime, directs the fine and large movements of the hand, arm, and shoulder. Thus, the eye carries thinking, feeling, and willing[3]; it registers vitality. The sense of life is connected to thinking[4]. As the sense of life helps convey thought into deed, it balances (with the support of the sense of balance) what the arm does, and moves (the sense of self-movement) the shoulder into action—for example, when aiming an arrow or a spear at a goal. The eye movements in their sockets are very similar to shoulder movements (the upper arm in the ball-and-socket shoulder joint). The child's pointing at an object or person at fourteen months is the precursor of the young person shaking hands while establishing eye contact.[5]

Hand Development in Infancy

The healthy newborn infant has such a strong hand grasp that her weight can be carried when she is lifted by the doctor whose fingers her two hands are grasping in a reflexive manner. Gradually, over the first year of development the infant's hands become able to let go of the finger that has stimulated the grasp reflex, and can then purposefully grasp an object she wants. The process by which a child gains his abilities to use the hands in more and more controlled ways is universal—if the child has an intact nervous system and is given the right environmental opportunities, it will seek to use its hands in more and more complex ways. Of course, how the child deals with his environment depends a great deal upon the child himself. The human being is not solely determined by heredity and environment.[6]

If the young infant's caregivers give her the opportunity to lie flat on her back during waking hours, you might observe how she rotates her hands in the air above her face, as if her hands were playing with the beams of light. The intent connecting of the eyes with what the hands are doing during this peaceful activity gives a wonderful foundation for future eye-hand con-

nections. The infant feels her hands' movements through her sense of self-movement (proprioception), she sees the play of light and dark as her hands and fingers change position, she feels her hands meet—at the vertical midline, giving her a beginning awareness of the two sides of her body and leading over time to the development of bilateral integration. This seemingly simple activity of the infants' hands may be crucial to the development of manual dexterity. If the infant spends most of her waking hours carried around or propped in infant seats, strollers, swings, walkers, bouncers, or other contraptions, she misses the opportunity to lift her arms up in this way and gracefully move her hands and fingers while her eyes connect with their activity. It would be very challenging for a young infant who is propped up (as in an infant seat or stroller) to raise her hands up so she can "finger the light beams" while she intently watches her hands move; she simply won't do this in a propped position. Another drawback with a propped-up position for the infant has been pointed out by Carla Hannaford in *Smart Moves: Why Learning is Not All in Your Head*: "These seats keep the baby at a forty-five degree angle that inhibits active muscular movements either of the neck or core muscles (of the abdomen and back). Even though the baby's eyes are forward, because movement is inhibited the baby is not actively developing vision."

Throughout the early months the grasp reflex continues to be elicited via the touch receptors (sense of touch) in the palm; gradually the grasp becomes more relaxed. The process that allows the hand to relax its reflexive grasping involves the baby's gross motor movements on the floor. Usually, by three to four months old, the baby has rolled over and finds herself on her stomach. Soon thereafter she starts to push on her hands to help raise her large and heavy head and shoulders up so she can look around from this new position. The pressure thus exerted onto her hands, as they gradually open up while she pushes down onto the floor, gives firm tactile input onto her palms. Because this tactile input happens while she carries weight on her palms she cannot easily respond by closing her fingers around this tactile sensation—her grasp response fades away naturally. This pressure on the palms continues as she creeps around on her hands and knees.

In the school-aged child who is asked to creep like a baby you often see that the fingers curl under as the child does not put his weight fully onto the palms of the hands. Sometimes a child places the knuckles of the fisted hands onto the floor while creeping, in a stronger avoidance of contacting the palms to the floor. In both of these situations the child has probably not spent enough time creeping on hands and knees nor pushing onto the floor while lying prone as an infant; a residual palmar reflex is still active. These are usually the children who hold a pencil, crayon, and eating utensils in tense, awkward ways. Some also avoid contacting the palms to the substance they are working with while doing craft activities or kneading dough, for instance; you can see how they use their finger tips while working with their hands, in avoidance of having the palms touch anything.

By about the fifth month the infant can consciously, though still with difficulty, let go of an object. As the infant learns to stretch his fingers, coordination between bending and stretching develops; by eight months he can freely let go of an object when the hand is resting on a surface and by one year the object can be released in the air. The grasp-release function is now under control. Playing give and take games supports this development. When the infant, from eight months to a year, amuses himself by dropping everything onto the floor, he is practicing this capacity. He is also experiencing how long it takes for an object to hit the floor—subconsciously learning to gauge distances through his hearing, and what kind of sound the object makes against the floor—subconsciously learn-

ing the denseness of various substances. These "applied physics" lessons are subtly absorbed by the child.[7]

Again, given well functioning senses and plenty of opportunities to manipulate differently shaped, weighted, and textured objects in the environment, the development of the grasp follows a certain sequence. Initially the infant only grasps an object if it touches his palm; the three ulnar fingers (little, fourth, and middle fingers) then flex against the palm (ulnar-palmar grasp). At first the index finger and the thumb do not fully take part in this action. When the infant grasps with one hand the other will simultaneously, reflexively, clench. After a few months the index finger and thumb become more involved and you see a radial-palmar grasp. By about the fifth month both hands can be used to grasp objects simultaneously. Eventually the infant can use all fingertips (the pads of the fingers) against the pad of the thumb to grasp, without having to press the object against the palm. Finger coordination improves and gradually the infant can use one hand without a corresponding movement of the other, unless the movement involves new movement sequences or new objects. From using all finger pads the ability to use only the thumb and index finger pads develops through practice and exposure to a variety of objects to manipulate.

When the infant wants to grasp an object, the sequence of stretching-grasping development also follows a definite pattern. At first the arm, hand, and fingers are stretched to the maximum before the object is grasped, over-stretching in relation to the size of the object. As the coordination improves, the stretching will occur at the last moment, and the hand opens just enough to grasp that particular object.

By the time the infant is one year old, she can pick up a little green pea lying on the high chair tray by using a "pincer grasp"—grasping the pea between the pads of the thumb and the index finger, putting it into her mouth, and letting go of it. Not long thereafter the grasp is between the tip of the index finger and the tip of the thumb, a superior pincer grasp, and the tiny object can be picked up without the hand being supported by the surface of the table.

Another factor in the development of fine motor skills is the integration of early movement patterns. For instance, it is difficult for a child whose head movements are intimately connected to her or his hand movements to use scissors or to develop a relaxed pencil grip. For the head and trunk to act as centered, relaxed, and stable foundations that support the fine motor activities of the hand, the early movement patterns need to have matured. This maturation takes place naturally as the infant, toddler, and young child rolls, wiggles, crawls (on the stomach with the big toes providing the "push-off"), creeps (on knees and flat hands), walks, climbs, and eventually runs through space which is safe and which gives plenty of opportunity for unhindered movements (except for "obstacle courses" which children can squeeze, wiggle, inchworm, climb, and roll their way through). This gross motor development is equally important as it provides the postural basis for the development of a relaxed, mature pencil grip. Similarly, the integration of the grasp reflex (mentioned above) takes place naturally as the infant and young child crawls and creeps around, and as she or he engages the hands in more and more complex activities.

Development of Postural Control in the First Year

When lying on her back the young baby does not have to engage her senses or muscles to control her posture; the surface she is lying on supports her completely. Therefore she can fully engage in what her hands are doing as they freely move above her face. Gradually, as the control of her postural muscles increases, from the head downwards, she gains the ability to move her body in large motor movements. First she raises her head against gravity, either from a supine or

prone position. Eventually she rolls over from her back to her stomach, and then from her stomach to her back—that is if she is given the opportunity to spend plenty of time lying flat on her back.

Later she can drag herself forward on her belly, using her hands and legs like a human lizard, to get a toy that attracts her attention. Somehow she figures out how to push herself into a sitting position; she gains more and more balance as she falls over, pushes her trunk upright again, then just sits there flapping her arms up and down with delight. After her balance has improved in sitting, she gains enough trunk stability to be able to reach out toward a toy, grasp it, and manipulate it without falling over any more. This trunk stability is essential as a foundation for the hands' ability to develop their fine motor skills.

As the months pass, the infant figures out how to get onto hands and knees from sitting or lying prone, and then she rocks forward and back in this position. From this rocking forward and back, she develops the ability to creep backward and forward on her hands and knees. As we know, the ability to pull oneself up into standing and thereafter to walk, first along furniture and then freely, is universally human. Through crawling, creeping, and walking, the child explores, gets to know, and makes an internal imprint, or map, of three-dimensional space. This connection with space is critical for developing future abilities in school, not just for games, gymnastics, dance, and sports, but, in order to orient to the two-dimensional page when writing, calculating, and reading.

In the gradual development of postural control the infant will initially be able to perform only one function at a time. At first the infant can lie on her back and grasp an object; when she has rolled over and can lie on her stomach, she works on lifting her head up and stabilizing its posture before she can grasp a toy. After she can sit up, she spends time stabilizing her posture in this position before she grasps one object; eventually she can grasp an object, drop it, and grasp another. Finally she can hold an object with one hand, while the other hand reaches for something else.

The stages of movement development which lead the infant into uprightness and walking out of her own efforts are the signature of the ego helping the individual to find her way into her body and into three-dimensional space. If the infant has been allowed to accomplish these archetypal steps of maturing into her body out of her own efforts, without interference from her environment, the ego has been able to leave a deeper imprint than if she was continually "aided" by those around her.[8]

The steps involved in this archetypal movement development also lead to a gradual control of the postural system. When she struggles on her own, the infant is gradually readied to take on each new ability. Her balance is steadier, her postural system is more controlled: it is not at the mercy of unnecessary tensions in compensation for her inability to perceive what each of her postural senses tell her.

How Children Draw and Write

An 18-month-old toddler "drawing" (scribbling) with a stick crayon holds it in a fisted hand (cross palmar grasp), tip downward (on the little finger side), with the wrist slightly flexed and the forearm slightly supinated; the motion of the crayon across the paper (or wall?) is produced by shoulder and/or trunk movements.

A two- to three-year-old child holds the stick crayon with some differences: now the tip of the crayon is on the thumb side, the index finger begins to straighten and lie on top of the crayon, separating from the three other fingers which still grasp the crayon as a tight unit (partial cross palmar grasp); the forearm is pronated and the wrist is not flexed; the drawing motion is still guided by the movements of the shoulder and trunk. A block crayon is not held in this way; rather, the child grasps the block crayon with all

fingers pressing against it in a full cross palmar grasp, much like the younger child's grasp on a stick crayon.

After four years of age most children can hold the stick crayon or pencil through thumb opposition to the index and long fingers with the ring and small fingers in flexion beginning to stabilize the hand. As the ring and little fingers take up the role of stabilizing the hand against the drawing or writing surface, a subtle "arch" of the hand develops longitudinally from the wrist to the space between the base of the ring and long fingers. (Like the foot, the hand has two arches, a transverse and a longitudinal, which create a cross.) Gradually, small movements at the metacarpophalangeal and interphalangeal joints begin to control the movements of the crayon or pencil. The shoulder, elbow, forearm, and wrist act as stabilizing joints, along with the core muscles of abdomen and back, giving support and a firm foundation from which the finer movements of the hand and fingers can operate.

By the time the child is five- to six-years-old, his or her hand development has matured to the point where he or she now can eat and draw with a mature, "adult" grasp. When writing, the mature hand rests on its side, stabilized by the little and ring fingers. The stick crayon or pencil is grasped in a relaxed, graceful manner with the ends of the curved thumb and index finger across from each other on top of the crayon, supported by the side of the long finger's distal phalange underneath the crayon. The upper end of the crayon or pencil rests against the base of the index finger. Intrinsic muscles of the hand cause motions in the small joints of the hand and fingers that create the writing motions, while wrist extension moves the pencil across the page to the right. Again, the shoulder, elbow, forearm, and wrist act as stabilizing joints. The trunk and head are kept in neutral position without leaning or twisting to the side, nor folding over the work at the table.

Activities Which Support Hand Development

In today's homes and classrooms, one can see that many grade school children have not completed the normal movement development of the hand. Some children need much catch-up, while for others more opportunity for fine motor activity seems to suffice. It's a good idea to check visual acuity if the school-aged child is truly struggling with fine motor skills; far- or near-sightedness can affect the development of eye-hand coordination. When hands act more like paws, the child might benefit from regular hand massage and even passive finger movement with nursery rhymes or songs—while you're at it, massage and play with the feet, too!

The importance of engaging the children in fine motor activities to give them the opportunity for catching up on this development must be conveyed to teachers in training, as well as to parents. I suggest establishing a "craft corner" at home where school-aged children have access to a variety of art and craft items with which to create any number of cards, gifts, works of art, and useful objects. Supply this corner with such items as beeswax, plasticine, clay, baker's clay, colored tissue paper, glue, scissors, colored construction paper, colored crayons and pencils, watercolor paint, plain white paper of differing thickness and size, wooden or bamboo skewers, origami paper, yarn of various thickness and colors, sewing needles, knitting needles, crochet hooks, colored fleece, carding tools, glitter, lace paper, rice and textured paper, beads of various sizes and shapes, leather thong and leather scraps, fabric scraps, string, and rope. For example, the children can "finger knit" belts, felt wool fleece into flat pieces usable as potholders or trivets, sew a felt purse, fold origami figures, or tie ropes with different knots. Felting and modeling with large pieces of beeswax or clay is particularly helpful for children who tend to hold their hands fisted. Initially supervised access to pieces of wood, nails, screws, and a few good tools—hammer, saw, pliers, and screwdriver—which they can learn to use is also important. Activities in the garden, such as digging, raking, planting, weeding, and harvesting are invaluable experiences, not only for sensory and motor development of the hands, fingers, arms, and the whole body, but also for learning about nature and our interdependence with it.

A fun and challenging way to support fine motor development is learning to eat with chopsticks. One can let a younger child try to eat with chopsticks any way she can, then show the child who is five years or older how chopsticks are held in the countries where people use them on a daily basis. Hold them so that the little and ring fingers stabilize the lower chopstick in the base of the "valley" between the thumb and index finger, while the tip of the thumb together with the index and long fingers allow the upper chopstick to move against the stable lower one. The value of having the young and school-aged child participate in all the activities of the home, especially the kitchen, must not be forgotten. Of course, everything takes much longer when the little ones want to "help out", but the opportunity for education of the sensory and motor systems cannot be duplicated. The child not only furthers the maturation of the hand, but develops many important faculties in the process of opening a jar or bottle, turning a tight faucet, beating an egg by hand while holding the bowl with the other hand, cracking (and eventually separating) an egg, wringing out a wet rag, washing a dirty pot, folding a T-shirt neatly, dusting under a vase which is lifted up by the other hand, sweeping the kitchen floor (using sweeping motions across the vertical midline), grating the carrot with one hand while the other firmly holds the grater, cutting apple and orange slices, measuring the flour, kneading the bread dough by hand, pressing the pastry dough into the pie pan, cracking nuts, or any of the activities of the home.

The development of the feet is even more forgotten in today's world; we take the feet quite for granted and are surprised when they ache, become flat, or develop hammer-toes. Yet, the potential for the capacities of the foot is such that people who lose the use of their hands can perform most of the functions of the hands with their feet, such as brushing their teeth, writing, drawing, and painting. Our traditional childhood culture has foot games such as "This Little Piggy Went to Market" as a reminder that the development of the feet is not to be taken for granted or neglected. Foot clapping games where the parent takes the child's feet and moves them up and down at the ankles, wiggles the toes, or claps the soles together, while saying a nursery rhyme, delight little children and help connect them to their feet. Eventually the child can pick up little objects, scarves or marbles with their toes and put them in a basket. Walking on the toes like fairies, on the heels or on the outside of the soles like gnomes, or bunching up a sock underneath the foot by pulling at it with toes curling and straightening are other ideas for supporting toe and foot development. Rudolf Steiner reminded the first Waldorf teachers that it is important to look at children's feet when their hands have difficulties with handwriting. He suggested that school-aged children be taught to write with their feet (the child uses the foot of the dominant side). Class teachers who have used this approach have noticed that children's handwriting indeed does improve and that their fingers and hands become less tense.

Today's children are allowed to spend too many hours in front of video game, computer, and television screens for the fine movements of the hands and postural control to develop fully. Many adults seem to feel that the interaction of computer games and other electronic activities where children use their fingers on buttons and sticks is good enough for the development of eye-hand coordination and fine motor skills. But compare these hand motions with the ones children use when engaged in some of the activities suggested above. Who wants to see the development of the hand go in the direction of being able to perform fewer skilled motions and possibly just turn into an extension of the machine? I strongly urge all adults who work with children to take up the task of supporting the proper development of the hand. The hand with its ability to create and to freely give is what makes us truly human.

About the fine motor movements of the hand and fingers, professor Matti Bergström, a Finnish neuro-physiologist and author, says: "The brain discovers what the fingers explore. The density of nerve endings in our fingertips is enormous. Their discrimination is almost as good as that of our eyes. If we don't use our fingers, if in childhood and youth we become "finger-blind," this rich network of nerves is impoverished—which represents a huge loss to the brain and thwarts the individual's all-around development. Such damage may be likened to blindness itself. Perhaps worse, while a blind person may simply not be able to find this or that object, the finger-blind cannot understand its inner meaning and value. If we neglect to develop and train our children's fingers and the creative form-building capacity of their hand muscles, then we neglect to develop their understanding of the unity of things; we thwart their esthetic and creative powers. Those who shaped our age-old traditions always understood this. But today, Western civilization, an information-obsessed society that overvalues science and undervalues true worth, has forgotten it all. We are "value-damaged." The philosophy of our upbringing is science-centered and our schools are programmed toward that end. These schools have no time for the creative potential of the nimble fingers and hand, and that arrests the all-round development of our children—and of the whole community."

A Note on Block and Stick Crayons

Try drawing with a block crayon, then with a stick crayon, and notice the difference in your own posture and in the drawing. Which seems to create more tension in shoulders, neck, and hand? What is the history of the block crayon? There were no block crayons during Rudolf Steiner's time; they were not "invented" until the 1950s. I have heard from retired Waldorf teachers that two art teachers in a northern German Waldorf school designed the block crayons for artistic use in the upper grades. They were intended as a means of extending artistic techniques after the shaded drawing technique had been mastered in the first three grades. These types of drawings could not yet be made by kindergarten and lower grade school children whose hand, wrist, and arm development is still maturing. The typical forms drawn by young children are lines: at first scribbled lines, then "wooly balls," circles, spirals, triangles, and squares—which are all more readily drawn with stick crayons than with blocks. The block crayon delays the fine motor development of the hand, discourages the drawing of these archetypal forms of early childhood drawings, and causes many children to hurriedly complete a picture as they cover the paper with quick, broad strokes. When holding a block crayon the five- to six-year-old's hand is mostly pronated. There is little stabilizing effect of the flexed ring and little fingers, so the hand lacks full support and the motion of the crayon across the paper is mostly guided by the arm moving at the elbow and shoulder and/or the trunk leaning or twisting to the sides. This is quite a different picture from the hand holding a stick crayon or pencil, more reminiscent of a younger child who directs the crayon across the page with the help of the whole arm and/or trunk.

Many of today's kindergarten teachers who have stick crayons in their classrooms have noticed that the children draw more universal and age-typical pictures with more of the mentioned archetypes. In my work with second graders I have noticed how much longer they spend on drawing person-house-tree pictures when they use stick crayons and no block crayons. In my ob-

servation, they work with greater care and draw more archetypal forms.

Note: For those unfamiliar with anatomical terminology: phalanges are the bones of the fingers and the interphalangeal joints the joints between these bones. The metacarpophalangeal joints are between the bones of the hands (metacarpals) and the proximal (closest to the palms) phalanges. The distal phalanges are those of the ends of the fingers (furthest away from the palms). The pronated forearm turns the palm down while the supinated forearm turns the palm upward.

Endnotes

1   Frank Wilson, *The Hand: How its use shapes the brain, language, and human culture* (New York, Pantheon, 1998).

2   Rudolf Steiner, *Practical Advice to Teachers,* Lectures 4 and 7 (Rudolf Steiner Press, 1996).

3   Susan Greenfield, *The Human Brain: A Guided Tour* (Basic Books, New York, 1998).

4   Rudolf Steiner, *Man as a Being of Sense and Perception* (Rudolf Steiner Press, London, 1981); Karl König, A *Living Physiology*; Albert Soesman, *Our Twelve Senses* (Hawthorne Press, 1999).

5   Wilson, *The Hand.*

6   Michaela Glöckler, M. D., "Human Biography and its Genetic Instrument," Volume IV, Number 2, June, 1999, *Research Bulletin,* Waldorf Education Research Institute.

7   Stephen Edelglass et al., *The Marriage of Sense and Thought* (Lindisfarne, 1997).

8   Audrey McAllen, *The Extra Lesson* (Rudolf Steiner College Press, Sacramento, 1998); Joan Salter, *The Incarnating Child,* (Hawthorne Press, 1990); Magda Gerber, *Your Self-Confident Baby* (John Wiley and Sons, 1998).

෨෧

Ingun Schneider was a class teacher at the Sacramento Waldorf School for many years. She now directs the Remedial Education Training Program at Rudolf Steiner College in Fair Oaks, California.

Toward Human Development:
The Physiological Basis of Sleep

Lisa Gromicko

"A child will flourish if there is a regular rhythm between the will working during the day when it is awake and the will building up the growing organism in sleep. Then the body can become that instrument for which the child was already longing before birth."

—Norbert Glas, M.D.[2]

The human body is truly a work in progress, even into old age. We have the capacity to grow, to develop, and to create throughout life, but much depends upon the foundation that is laid in the period from birth to about seven years of age, when the child begins to lose the baby teeth. During this time, the basis of our humanity is formed. "The development of the physical body between birth and the change of teeth is the basis for the unfolding of the consciousness soul, that member of your soul-being in which the I first becomes revealed, between the ages of thirty-five to forty-two years" (McAllen).[3] Indeed, throughout life, every human action—impulse transformed into deed, every thought, and word spoken is sounded through and limited by the physical body that is developed in the first seven years of life. The capacity of the child to learn in grade school through the awakened cognitive senses, for example, presupposes the well-developed nerve-sense-brain and the lower-will senses (life, touch, movement, and balance)

in early childhood.[4] The early growth years are crucial. And if we look harder at this enormous work of the young human being, we find that the only time that physical growth occurs is during sleep. In addition, sleep is the only time that the body restores and renews its forces from the demands of the day. So, why don't children sleep all of the time?

Young children are completely sense beings. We can even step back and say that sensation forms the embryo.[5] Through the *gates of the senses*, life forces flow. These cosmic forces are then "orchestrated" by the ego (the I) into physical matter. The myriad physiological systems are thus established. (The nerve-sense organs, brain, and nervous system can only be stimulated to form better during the first eight to nine years, after this time, their forming activity stops.[6] The circulatory, metabolic, and skeletal systems take longer.) "The nervous system develops through physical movement."[7] The infant and the young child are totally given over to the environment, extending themselves into it, and actually *consuming* every single detail of life that meets the senses. Every color, smell, sound, taste, texture, word, shape, activity, and even the moods of others—everything is taken in. "Every psychic stimulus passes over into the circulation, the breath, the digestion. Body, soul, and spirit are still unity. This is why every stimulus from the environment passes right down into the child's bodily nature." [8] But, ". . . because he is not yet in the position to catch and digest the sense impressions with consciousness, so can they penetrate without hindrance directly into the child's organism."[9] Yet, this is what forms the basis of physical development. What the child receives through the senses will become the child's physical body. It is also the reason why care and protection are so essential to provide healthy impressions as well as the avoidance of over-stimulation. "Assaults to the nerve/sensory system while it is being formed give the same damage as encephalitis."[10]

In sleep, the *food* (impressions) of the senses are literally digested through the metabolism and are then transformed into the physical forming of the organs, brain-nerve-sense pathways, endocrine system, circulatory-rhythmic, lower senses, digestion, skeletal, the entire physical constitution. This occurs under the direction of the ego through the etheric (life) forces. The etheric forces give life, form, energy, and health to the body, working strongly in the immune system and in all growth and repairing processes. These are the forces that dominate from birth to the change of teeth.[11] But, we also know that it is in sleep that the etheric body itself is renewed. This seems contradictory, but the renewal process is due to the cosmic nature of the etheric life body and to the spiritual realm of sleep. According to Rudolf Steiner, although the overall time spent in sleep is shorter, the "evolution" of the sleep life is more significant in many respects than that of waking life. "For the whole condition of the human being, above all for the gaining and maintenance of health and hence for earthly life as a whole. . ."[12] The physical body is the vessel for the higher members of the human being. Loving care and reverence for its development opens the door to the child's destiny. It is in sleep that children meet their angels.[13]

The day's sense impressions are taken into sleep, forming the content that is used by the etheric to build up the physical body and at the same time, restoring essential life forces. How does this occur? The primary organ of the etheric is the liver. It is the dominant metabolic organ in the fetus (with the thymus) and in all growth processes in life. "It is the place of general substance formation and of the origin of human substance. In terms of substance, the process of becoming man occurs in the liver."[14] The liver is also tremendously significant in the young child because it is the organic basis of the *will*. Its proper development has far-reaching consequences in the life of the individual. "For you must know that the liver is not merely the organ modern physiology describes; it is pre-eminently the organ that gives the human being the courage to transform a deed which has been thought of into an accomplished deed."[15] For the school-age child, sufficient healthy sleep also supports metabolic processes that are responsible for "working over what was comprehended to the point at which the memory can retain it."[16]

The liver's vitalizing-restorative, growth related processes occur in deep sleep. Its functions are plant-like in the human being and follow a *rhythmic* sleep-wake cycle. This is very important. Sensations from the day are received by the sympathetic nervous system and are *imitated* or *reacted to* (if stressful) by the metabolism, which secretes into the lymph, response substances by the impacted organ(s). These secretions may be digestive fluids, insulin, adrenaline, cortisol (stress hormones), epinephrine, etc. They are *sensed* by the liver and form a kind of fluid stimulus record which, through the building-up processes of the etheric during sleep, become transformed into the lung, heart, kidney, nervous system, brain, the liver itself, etc. Carbohydrates are synthesized into sugars (glycogen), which are then stored in the liver during its "night" assimilatory phase beginning at about 3:00 p.m. and peaking at about 3:00 a.m. These stored sugars are converted to blood glucose during the daytime for the activities of consciousness beginning at 3:00 a.m., through the catabolic

58

(breaking down) influence of the gall bladder in the liver until about 3:00 p.m. Here, we can see the importance of going to sleep early: 6:30-8:00 p.m. for children and 9-10:00 p.m. for adults. Staying up late causes the liver to reverse its storing-up activity intended for the next day and to instead begin converting glycogen to glucose for energy, thus we get a "second wind" (especially children). This explains the worn-out feeling the next morning and the daylong physiologic struggle to "keep up."[17]

"Life continues during sleep, and the forces that are active and creative during the waking state receive their strength and renewal from what is given to them by sleep. . . human being who does not continually draw strength for his weakened forces from sleep must of necessity destroy his life."[18] The catabolic breakdown (awake) phase of the gall-liver is a *destructive* process that is necessary for consciousness. The incarnation of the individual into earthly substance requires "fire" or warmth (to carry the Ego), and air. Beginning at birth, this condition is created in the oxidative, combustion breakdown of formative substance (prepared by the liver in sleep), releasing warmth. (It isn't until about 9 years of age that the child can regulate his warmth organism.) The awake/breakdown phase is related to the nerve-sense system, whose proper function and development eventually leads to the *thinking* capacities beginning after the change of teeth. At that time, formative growth forces are then metamorphosed into intellectual forces. During sleep is the only time that the nervous system can rest, repair, and build up. During waking hours, there is "no possibility for new cell growth."[19] The destructive forces of consciousness (nerve-sense system) are balanced by the restorative forces of sleep (liver-metabolic system). These two systems are mediated by the rhythmic system. The sleep-wake rhythm supports human growth and consciousness.

"Everything of a rhythmical nature contains a special force."[20] Rhythm is the balance between the life processes of rest and movement. The physiologic representative of this balance is the heart, the primary organ of the rhythmic system. The cardiovascular system, in particular the heart, is the mediator between the nerve-sensory system and the metabolic system. In the dynamics of these three physiologic systems, we can see the inter-related rhythms of sleeping, breathing, birth and death. In the contracting events of awakening, inspiration, and systole are the incarnating tendencies of the nervous system. In the expanding events of falling asleep, expiration, and diastole are the excarnating tendencies of metabolism. (In reality, the nerve senses are relatively still, cold, and deathlike. In comparison, the metabolic system is in full, active movement.) Rhythm exists as the third state as a result of the polar existence of rest and movement, something new. It brings the possibility for freedom. "In the human heart, the earthly and the cosmic are intimately united. . .Between rest and movement, space and time, form and substance tendency, systole and diastole, the human ego experience can develop in freedom experienced within. . .The heart muscle stands between the two, as is appropriate for feeling as a half-conscious soul capacity; conscious thinking is based on the nerve-sensory system and unconscious will on the metabolic system."[21] Rhythm truly is the carrier of life (Steiner). Healthy development of the heart and the rhythmic system is essential for life and is the physical basis for the unfolding of the *feeling* life beginning in adolescence.

Lack of a rhythmic lifestyle places great demands on the heart as the central organ of rhythm. Excessive stimulation, now part and parcel of modern life, creates inner, often constant unconscious stress, leading to "fight or flight" physiologic responses. The metabolism, by way of the adrenal glands, produces stress hormones such as adrenaline, cortisol, dopamine, and noradrenaline as a result of the strain on the nervous system.[22] In young children, fatigue produces the same metabolic response, causing wakefulness, irritability, and being generally wound-up. It can be very difficult then to calm down and to go to sleep. The more sleep-deprived a child is, the more excitable he will be, and some children in this condition are constantly in various states of arousal. The stress hormones produced in response to arousal tax the liver greatly. Blood pressure, breath, and heart rate accelerate, as well as many other processes, which the heart as *central* to the rhythmic system must mediate. Over time, this can become pathological and hence the increase today in cardiovascular (rhythmic) diseases. The "loss of the middle" (Steiner)[23] is a serious problem of our time as it represents the loss of the being of man. Physiologically, the organ most affected is the heart. But also spiritually speaking, the heart is the organ which is most related to the ego, the "I".[24] Many serious heart ailments in adults, as well as numerous other illnesses, have to do with the prolonged *inner* reaction of the physical body to the influences of stress, emotions, desires, anger (i.e. the forces of the astral) that damage the life processes. For the young child, over-stimulation, along with lack of sufficient sleep and rhythm compromise healthy physical development, setting the stage in adulthood for impaired life processes, with perhaps increased difficulty in mastering the astral forces. Improper development of the liver rhythm (sleeping-waking) is particularly detrimental in a child. Then "it is possible that the person will remain inactive despite his best intentions…If, despite proper initial development, the liver is not properly formed, then a will-defect develops that is expressed in the child's wanting to do something that does not pass over into the carrying out of the will impulse but remains stuck in thinking" (Steiner). This realization of the liver as an organ of the will is of the greatest significance for education, psychiatry, and therapy."[25]

Many cosmic and biological rhythms exist that affect the human being. For example, the rhythmical life sphere of the earth's organism was described by scientist Gunther Wachsmuth

(1893-1963), who called it the "respiration sphere."[26] This sphere of the earth's life (etheric) forces affects atmospheric, meteorological patterns, and all life on the planet. Its supersensible existence is expressed in several interesting phenomena. The "semi-diurnal atmospheric pressure wave" caresses the earth rhythmically twice in each twenty-four-hour period, moving like a mighty wave around the planet. This brings about high pressures at 9:00 a.m./9:00 p.m. (in breath) and low pressures at 3:00 a.m./ 3:00 p.m. (out breath). There are also corresponding electrical and magnetic occurrences. The electric potential between the atmosphere and the earth's surface, as well as the oscillations of the earth's magnetic field have the same respective high and low points/phases. In addition, compass readings of magnetic North are strongly deflected to the East at 9:00, and at 3:00 return to the West. "Human life is influenced by the rhythm of the sphere of forces. In the morning, from 8:00 to 10:00 the human being is most efficient. From about midday on, there is a "sleepy" crisis, lasting until about three. Following this, a phase of mental awakening begins which reaches a high point at around 9:00 p.m. and then fades away again later in the evening. A repeated crisis at 3:00 a.m. is not usually noticed by a sleeping human being, but is the hour when night-workers have greatest difficulty in keeping awake. This ebb of energy is also reflected by the fact that it is often the time of human death. These rhythmical effects of the sphere of forces mould important life processes, even in the formation of the embryo, and strongly influence the nature of the human being like a pulse acting from without that infiltrates the basic framework of the human constitution."[27] Dr. Michaela Glöckler, M.D. speaks about the same physiological rhythms of the school child when she states that, "In school, children tend to be alert in the morning, but then are all tired out between 1:00 and 2:30 p.m. when they experience a sharp decline in their physiologic activity. In the later afternoon, there is a second peak when they are happy and like to be active, and then a second decline before the later evening when they want to sleep."[28] Each of these rhythms corresponds to the liver, sleep-wake rhythm.

"In sleep, the organism returns to the activities that came at the starting point of its development, in the embryonic period and early infancy. In the waking state, processes coming at the end of human development, processes of aging and dying, predominate."[29] In consideration of healthy physical development, one cannot stress enough the need for long periods of rest and sleep for young children. In fact, due to the increasing pace of life, *more* sleep is needed now than ever before to offset the physiologic strain on the young body. "Small, but constant deficits in sleep over time tend to have escalating and perhaps long-term effects on brain function. . . Some learning disabilities and Attention Deficit Hyperactivity Disorder (ADHD) are attributed in part to sleep deprivation."[30] (Interestingly, ADHD is then treated with stimulant medications.) Immune function is also lowered. In addition, the developing lower senses are seriously affected. The child's *sense of life* is diminished by a shortage of sleep. Through the life sense, the child can experience feeling well in his body, that the world is good. "In the sense of life we experience all our metabolic processes, all the forces which build and form our body. All of this is experienced as a kind of well being so long as we are well. The sense of life for us is a happy sense, a happy experience."[31] But, it is the sense of touch, the sense of "bodily form and extension," which suffers most from the lack of sleep. "The sensation we have of being enclosed in a sheath, we owe to the processes taking place in sleep." Without an adequate feeling of "boundary," given by the sense of touch, the child is exposed or "thin-skinned," and consequently over-sensitive and awkward in space.[32]

So, how much sleep do children need?[33]

Newborn	16 hours
8 mos. to 1 year	15 hours
1½ to 2 years	14 hours
4 to 5 year	12 hours
6 to 7 years	11 hours
8 to 9 years	10-11 hours
10 years	10 hours
14 years	8 hours or more

(depending on timing of rapid growth spurts)

For young children, these sleep amounts include naptimes. Naps are extremely beneficial. "Long naps occurring at the right times make the child feel rested. . . A missed nap is sleep lost forever."[34] Children do not make up their naps at night, just as they do not make up a good night's sleep in the morning. They are beings of the sun and are healthiest when they go to bed early and "rise with the sun." Naps allow a child's nervous system much needed rest. The type of nap-sleep varies according to the time of day. Morning naps have more REM (rapid eye movement) sleep and help with brain maturation (in early life). This nap is dropped first. The afternoon nap has more non-REM sleep, which is more important for physical restoration.[35] Non-REM (quiet) sleep is characterized by slow brain waves of high amplitude, regular, deep respiration, slow, rhythmic heart rate, some muscular tone, and lower blood pressure than in waking states. A greater percentage of this stage is experienced with increasing age. REM sleep is characterized by irregular, high frequency brain waves, involuntary muscular twitches, rapid eye movements associated with dreaming, shallow respiration, rapid heart rate, and variable blood pressure. Infants and young children spend about half their sleeping time in REM sleep that correlates with physical growth.[36] Growth hormone (GH) levels rise sharply during sleep,[37] but some research shows that GH levels are lowered by elevated cortisol (a stress hormone), reasserting the previously stated need to protect the developing nerve-sense system of the young child and to provide more sleep.

Children who do not nap have elevated stress hormones that also cause increased alertness and irritability. The nap should last for at least thirty minutes (an hour is better) and is best spent in a stationary place (not in a car, rocking chair, etc.). Afternoon naps need to end by 2:30 or 3:00 p.m. at the latest. The liver begins its night restorative phase at that time and sleeping later than 3:00 displaces the night-time sleep, causing the child to have difficulty falling asleep by 7:00 or 8:00 p.m. According to Philip Incao, M.D., ". . .the more hours of sleep before midnight, the better. Sleep after 3:00 a.m. is less restorative because of the liver rhythm, which begins its wakeful-will-stimulating (more active flow of bile) mode from 3:00 a.m. to 3:00 p.m., roughly."[38] Interestingly for children, the more regular sleep that they get, the easier it is to fall asleep. "Children who are not overtired sleep much better and more quietly at night," writes Norbert Glas, M.D.[39] Children ages three to six still need a nap of one to three hours. A child of five to six years may give up the nap if she is regularly going to bed early, by around 7:00 p.m., and is not showing signs of sleep-deprivation which for children are the opposite of those shown by adults. Instead of yawning and becoming quieter, children become more excitable. Inda Schaenen, author of *The 7 O'Clock Bedtime*, makes a strong case for a 7:00 bedtime and says that once the parent determines how much sleep the child needs, this need becomes "nonnegotiable."[40] Although some may not sleep, all children including "non-sleepers," benefit from an enforced rest-time. Being able to pause (to be still and quiet) is a skill that eludes even many adults. Children need desperately to learn this. As always, a fair amount of firm inner conviction is required of the adult to secure for the child what he needs.

"Before age nine, the most important thing is for children to learn how to properly sleep" (Steiner).[41] Audrey McAllen describes sleeping as a "breathing rhythm between the soul-spirit and the earthly body." She adds that learning to sleep and learning to eat, "to take in substance and transform it, an action of the ego" are the two most "important educational factors" in the life of the young child.[42] As we have seen, the transformation of substance, whether it is through the digestion of food or sensory impressions occurs on the physiologic level by way of the liver metabolism during sleep. How do we teach children to sleep properly? The breathing image given by Audrey McAllen is the key. Learning to sleep is learning to breathe. Without rest, the human being is continually breathing in. We are really speaking about a rhythmic function. Rhythm is living, breathing, life giving, never exactly the same, but regular. The young child's rhythmic (cardiovascular) system is not yet developed, but the health and building up of the entire physiology depends upon rhythm. Rhythm must be imprinted in the early years from without. The child learns to sleep by having adults that understand the profound importance of sleep. Sacrifices are usually necessary today to create a rhythmic lifestyle that allows for an unhurried pace. This includes regulating when the child sleeps and awakens, mealtimes, when and how much play, limiting stimulation, consistency, predictability—a slow, even tempo with rests at regular intervals. The quality of sense impressions that are ingested during the day also have a tremendous influence on the child's ability to sleep.[43] Heavy meals after 3:00 p.m. are a burden for the liver, which begins its night regenerative phase then. A special nightly ritual before bedtime such as a candle with a simple story, and a prayer or verse is golden food for sleep. This forming of the day, week, month, and year by the adult creates habits in the young child that literally form the physiological systems (particularly the rhythmic system), as well as future habits and the capacity to adapt. A sleep-habit life is thus developed which provides the basis for more sleep. The child then lives securely within real limits and form, a kind of swaddling that engenders trust, happiness, and healthy development of the nerve-sense, rhythmic, and metabolic systems. This establishes the foundation for the higher capacities of thinking, feeling, and willing.[44] Sleep provides growth and life renewing processes as well as the bridge to becoming truly human.

Bibliography

Aeppli, Willi. *The Care and Development of the Human Senses*. Sussex, U.K.: Steiner Waldorf Schools Fellowship, 1993.

Falck-Ytter, Harald. *Aurora. The Northern Lights in Mythology, History, and Science*. Great Britain: Bell Pond Books, 1999.

Fried, Richard. Lecture: *Sleep and the Young Child*. Kimberton Waldorf School, October 7, 1999.

Glas, Norbert. *Conception, Birth, & Early Childhood*. Spring Valley, NY: Anthroposophic Press, 1983.

Glöckler, Michaela, M.D. *A Healing Education. How Can Waldorf Education Meet the Needs of Children?* Fair Oaks, CA.: Rudolf Steiner College Press, 2000.

Glöckler, Michaela, M.D. *"The Birth of the Etheric." A Deeper Understanding of the Waldorf Kindergarten*, Vol. 2. Waldorf Kindergarten Association, 1993.

Glöckler, Michaela, M.D. "Forces of Growth and Forces of Fantasy." *A Deeper Understanding of the Waldorf Kindergarten*, Vol. 2. Waldorf Kindergarten Association, 1993.

Husemann, Friedrich and Otto Wolff. *The Anthroposophical Approach to Medicine, Vol. 2*. Hudson, NY: Anthroposophic Press, 1982.

Incao, Philip. Letter. May 24, 2002.

Jensen, David. *The Principles of Physiology*. New York: Appleton-Century-Crofts, 1976.

Johnson, Susan R. "The Importance of Sleep." *You and Your Child's Health*—series of articles. Fair Oaks, CA.: Raphael House.

Klocek, Dennis. "The Young Child from Birth to Seven." *Gateways—A Newsletter of the Waldorf Early Childhood Association of North America*. Spring/Summer 2001, Issue 40, pp. 4-11.

Kohler, Henning. *Working with Anxious, Nervous, and Depressed Children*. Fair Oaks, CA.: The Association of Waldorf Schools of North America, 2000.

Konig, Karl. A *Living Physiology*. Great Britain: Camphill Books, 1999.

McAllen, Audrey E. *Sleep*. Gloucestershire, U.K.: Hawthorne Press, 1981.

Poplawski, Thomas. "Etheric? Astral? Ego? An Esoteric View of the Human Being and its Value in the Education of the Child." *Renewal. A Journal for Waldorf Education*, Spring-Summer 2002.

Schaenen, Inda. *The 7 O'Clock Bedtime*. New York, NY: Harper Collins, 2001.

Spitalny, Stephen. "Characterizing and Balancing Polarities:Some Thoughts and Themes." *Gateways. A Newsletter of the Waldorf Early Childhood Association of North America*, Spring/Summer 2002.

Steiner, Rudolf. *An Outline of Occult Science*. Hudson, New York: Anthroposophic Press, 1972.

Steiner, Rudolf, *Balance in Teaching*. Spring Valley, New York: Mercury Press, 1982.

Steiner, Rudolf. *The Driving Force of Spiritual Powers in World History*. Great Britain: Bookprint International Ltd. England, 1972.

Steiner, Rudolf. *Lecture Course on Curative Education*, Volume 1, 1924. Dornach, Switzerland: Rudolf Steiner Nachlassverwaltung, 1952.

Steiner, Rudolf. *Physiology and Therapeutics*. Spring Valley, New York: Mercury Press, 1986.

Steiner, Rudolf. *Understanding Young Children*.

Excerpts from lectures by Rudolf Steiner, compiled for the use of kindergarten teachers. Stuttgart, Germany: International Association of Waldorf Kindergartens, 1975.

Steiner, Rudolf and Ita Wegman. *Extending Practical Medicine*. London: Rudolf Steiner Press, 1996.

Von Kugelgen, Helmut. "Working with the Angels, Archangels, and the Archai." A *Deeper Understanding of the Waldorf Kindergarten, Vol. 2.* Waldorf Kindergarten Association, 1993.

Weissbluth, Marc. *Healthy Sleep Habits, Happy Child*. New York, NY: Random House, Inc., 1999.

Endnotes

1 Frank Wilson, *The Hand: How its use shapes the brain, language, and human culture* (New York, Pantheon, 1998).

2 Norbert Glas, *Conception, Birth, & Early Childhood* (Spring Valley, NY: Anthroposophic Press, Inc., 1983), p. 76.

3 Audrey E. McAllen, *Sleep* (Gloucestershire, U.K.: Hawthorne Press, 1981), p. 18.

4 Willi Aeppli, *The Care and Development of the Human Senses* (Sussex, U.K.: Steiner Waldorf Schools Fellowship, 1993), p. 64.

5 Dennis Klocek, "The Young Child from Birth to Seven," *Gateways—A Newsletter of the Waldorf Early Childhood Association of North America*, Spring/Summer 2001, Issue 40, p. 4.

6 Michaela Glöckler, *A Healing Education. How Can Waldorf Education Meet the Needs of Children?* (Fair Oaks, CA: Rudolf Steiner College Press, 2000), p. 47.

7 Michaela Glöckler, "The Birth of the Etheric," *A Deeper Understanding of the Waldorf Kindergarten, Volume 2* (Waldorf Kindergarten Association of North America, 1993), p. 30.

8 Rudolf Steiner, *Understanding Young Children*. Excerpts from lectures by Rudolf Steiner, compiled for the use of kindergarten teachers (Stuttgart, Germany: International Association of Waldorf Kindergartens, 1975), p. 61.

9 Aeppli, p. 47.

10 Stephen Spitalny, "Characterizing and Balancing Polarities—Some Thoughts and Themes," *Gateways. A Newsletter of the Waldorf Early Childhood Association of North America*, Spring/Summer 2002, Issue 42, p. 13.

11 Thomas Poplawski, "Etheric? Astral? Ego? An Esoteric View of the Human Being and its Value in the Education of the Child," *Renewal. A Journal for Waldorf Education*, Volume II, no. 1, (Spring-Summer 2002), pp. 11-12.

12 Rudolf Steiner, *The Driving Force of Spiritual Powers in World History* (Great Britain: Bookprint International Ltd. England, 1972), pp. 3, 14.

13 Helmut von Kugelgen, "Working With the Angels, the Archangels, and the Archai," *A Deeper Understanding of the Waldorf Kindergarten, Volume 2* (Waldorf Kindergarten Association, 1993), p. 79.

14 Friedrich Husemann, and Otto Wolff, *The Anthroposophical Approach to Medicine, Volume 2* (Hudson, NY: Anthroposophic Press, 1982), p. 205.

15 Rudolf Steiner, *Lecture Course on Curative Education, Volume 1*, 1924 (Dornach, Switzerland: Rudolf Steiner Nachlassverwaltung, 1952), p. 1/9.

16 Rudolf Steiner, *Balance in Teaching* (Spring Valley, New York: Mercury Press, 1982), p. 34.

17 Susan R. Johnson, "The Importance of Sleep," *You and Your Child's Health*, (Fair Oaks, California: Raphael House).

18 Rudolf Steiner, *An Outline of Occult Science* (Hudson, NY: Anthroposophic Press, 1972),

pp. 48-49.

19 Glöckler, A *Healing Education*, p. 46.

20 Aeppli, p. 68.

21 Husemann and Wolff, pp. 319, 323.

22 Marc Weissbluth, *Healthy Sleep Habits, Happy Child* (New York, NY: Random House, Inc., 1999), pp. 64-65.

23 Husemann and Wolff, p. 390.

24 Husemann and Wolff, p. 394.

25 Husemann and Wolff, p. 214.

26 Harald Falck-Ytter, *Aurora. The Northern Lights in Mythology*, History, and Science (Great Britain: Bell Pond Books, 1999), p. 109.

27 Falck-Ytter, pp. 109-111.

28 Glöckler, A *Healing Education*, pp. 59-60.

29 Rudolf Steiner and Ita Wegman, *Extending Practical Medicine* (London: Rudolf Steiner Press, 1996), p. 63.

30 Weissbluth, pp. 47-48.

31 Karl Konig, A *Living Physiology* (Great Britain: Camphill Books, 1999), p. 107.

32 Henning Kohler, *Working with Anxious, Nervous, and Depressed Children* (Fair Oaks, California: The Association of Waldorf Schools of North America, 2000), pp. 58-59.

33 Richard Fried, Lecture: "Sleep and the Young Child," (Kimberton Waldorf School, October 7, 1999).

34 Weissbluth, pp. 27, 208.

35 Weissbluth, p. 25.

36 David Jensen, *The Principles of Physiology* (New York: Appleton-Century-Crofts, 1976), p. 433.

37 Jensen, p. 1031.

38 Letter received from Philip Incao, 24 May 2002.

39 Glas, p. 76.

40 Inda Schaenen, *The 7 O'Clock Bedtime* (New York, NY: Harper Collins, 2001), p. 6.

41 Michaela Glöckler, "Forces of Growth and Forces of Fantasy," A *Deeper Understanding of the Waldorf Kindergarten*, Volume 2 (Waldorf Kindergarten Association, 1993), p. 47.

42 McAllen, p. 24.

43 Glöckler, "Forces of Growth and Forces of Fantasy," A *Deeper Understanding of the Waldorf Kindergarten*, Vol. 2, p. 47. "The child is helped to sleep at night if it has been helped to awaken properly in the day. This occurs through the purposeful activities which the adult does in the child's presence during the day. The child needs to experience clarity and purposeful direction in the daytime. Then it experiences proper calm at night."

44 Rudolf Steiner, *Physiology and Therapeutics* (Spring Valley, NY: Mercury Press, 1986), p. 33.

⁀

After several years as the Kindergarten Aftercare Teacher at Kimberton Waldorf School, Lisa is currently working as Kindergarten Assistant there while another colleague is away on medical leave. She has completed her Master's in Early Childhood at Sunbridge College.

Laying the Physical Foundation of the Consciousness Soul

Dr. Jenny Josephson

How can we support child development between birth and seven so that the Consciousness Soul can develop fully between the ages of thirty-five to forty-two? This is a matter of present development working for the future. We can consider three important principles.

The state of the child and his relationship to his own higher members

At birth, the physical body is born but immature and not yet mastered. The other bodies are in embryonic form. The child lives in a created world—things just are. This is the world of the Father God, or greater God, "Thou shalt not." The child and the world are one. Gradually, independence comes about, but within our physical body, the world of childhood is written. This encompasses also the people in our world, together with their inner qualities.

The relationship of body and soul between birth and age seven

The soul is embryo-like within the child. It perceives and incorporates into itself physical bodily processes that are later to be transformed into soul process. We must look carefully at them. The soul is "watching" now in order to do later, and we must be responsible for what is observed. The physical body is a temple, reflecting the macrocosm both generally and individually,

and needs to have reverence and tremendous care. The wisdom of the human body is far greater than that of individual wisdom.

It is especially important to observe the child's gestures, e.g., his way of walking. This can be a part of the evening review where we can begin to see the essential being. This is living on the threshold between what is manifest to the senses and the spiritual. Humanity has crossed this threshold unknowingly and is continually encountering threshold experiences—there is a danger of losing control of thinking, feeling and willing.

Where every gesture counts, inwardness can bring the spiritual into any gesture. We can take consciousness into every deed, including being as skillful as possible. We can recognize in each individual a child of God. Care and love can enter all that we do, and then things will not fall into destruction. Whenever people are brought together in a relationship of love, we construct a spiritual architecture in which we will meet again after death. To continually live in such thoughts is the task of the age of the Consciousness Soul.

The principle of change

We need to remember that there is much development to come that is inevitable. In later life, the Consciousness Soul learns by overcoming. We must allow the child to overcome and not always hasten to take away the struggle.

We must cultivate in the child the joy of learning. When lessons become more personal, more individual, then we enter the realm of the childhood illnesses such as measles, mumps, whooping cough, and chicken pox. We must give time for illness and the joy of recovery.

Change means sacrifice. Fever in the small child is a sacrificial fire—it burns itself in order to move forward. The adult world has become frightened of fever, tending to judge illness instead of listening to it. It might be necessary for the child to produce illness in order to bring about change. The child may be fine, but his environment awful. Illness in small children may have to do with us. The question one may ask is, "Who needs to change, me or the child?"

There are two dangers. The first is medical technology where Ahriman slides in and takes away illness.

The second is arrogance under the excuse that illness is necessary. In this case, Lucifer takes hold in a different way. Therapeutically, both sides need to be brought together in a joining of extremes, which is one aspect of the Consciousness Soul.

How can we work? In the first seven years, the four lower senses are particularly important for the development of the child and for the Consciousness Soul. These bodily senses are portals for the soul/spirit nature to communicate with the physical world.

Touch: With this sense, we experience "Here I end"—the limit of ourselves. This leads to a trust in oneself, in the world and in destiny.

Well-being: This emphasizes the relationship of the whole to the parts and that the whole is greater than the sum of the parts. Sometimes we need to sacrifice personal destiny for the greater community. We struggle between the calls of personal and professional karma.

Movement: This awakens awareness of ones own activity. Movement leads to deeds, which cannot be undone. After each of the days of creation, God saw that it was good. We have the responsibility to do what we ought, because we can. (In the Kindergarten, after the age of five, we encourage the child to move from what he wants to do, to what he should do). With physical handicap, movement has to be achieved through struggle.

Balance: We are able to hold ourselves upright in three-dimensional space. Balance also brings the ability to weigh the extremes in our soul, the polarities of Lucifer and Ahriman. We can seek a balanced state-of-being even when life about us is unbalanced. Children need strong limbs (these limbs serve the Will forces). It is a tragedy that walking is no longer a part of daily life and that it is often not safe for children to run free. Movement can have many qualities, e.g., purpose, generosity. The kindergarten is a place to practice motor skills. Eurythmy in the kindergarten is an extra dimension and a gift for the future of individuals and humanity as a whole. It balances the mechanistic movement that surrounds us today.

These senses can be strengthened and used consciously in the service of spiritual development. Many of Rudolf Steiner's exercises start with sense perception. If we fail to cultivate the senses, we place a boulder before human development.

The senses are difficult to experience because they work together, but we can become more observant of them individually. (In her book *Nobody Nowhere*, Donna Williams describes her experience of autism. Each sense was like a pearl on a string, but they weren't working together. Her breakthrough with this experience is movingly described in a second book, *Somebody Somewhere*.) With these senses, a foundation is laid for soul-qualities. Certainty of self arises from these, e.g., from touch, from the I experience.

Well-being is a foundation for an understanding that the whole is greater than the sum of the parts. There needs to be wholeness in the atmosphere of the kindergarten. Saying and doing should form a whole—we need to speak the truth and remember that children are very literal. We need to strive to be appropriate in our questions of them and in our replies to their questions. Thinking, feeling and willing are parts of a whole, a three-leaf clover, with the four-leaf clover being the addition of the ego.

Movement offers freedom, but also responsibility. What is movement? In his book, *Under the Eye of the Clock*, Christopher Nolan, who is paralyzed, explores this question. "How do I conquer my body? Can a paralytic move?" From this questioning, we are led to the theme of a more inner, spiritual movement. Children need strong limbs to remain "upright," even though the ground is "rough," we can take this metaphorically. At the famous Vienna Riding School, the horses are taken into rocky pastures when young, then back to Vienna where they can then achieve almost impossible movements, for they have learned balance on the rough terrain. Children need also to experience the different qualities of movement, e.g., the fine motor skills involved in sewing, finger games, modeling. Eurythmy is also a great gift.

Touch introduces the experience of limitations. Children now desperately need new forms of limits, for they are no longer held by tradition. We ourselves need to develop awareness in order to support them, e.g., consistency and punctuality. Punctuality brings time and space together, which are the qualities of incarnation. This self-mastery gives our children new possibilities. Limits on behavior are needed to contain a child. Children test our limits and then re-test. Then they change and expect the limits to change. Adults need a strong will to meet today's children in addition to an artistic and creative approach to discipline.

We only have a short time with the child in the kindergarten. It is therefore imperative that we make contact with parents in order to realize the potential of our work. The child desperately needs this cooperation which can then cradle him or her in consistency.

This prayer is for a child who is far away or in special need:

Lord place your head on her shoulder
Speak to her ear
Whisper in her heart
Lead her the way she should go.

෨෨

Dr. Jenny Josephson has practiced anthroposophical medicine in England for many years. She has a special interest in the developing child. This article was from a talk given at the International Kindergarten Conference in England, September 1995 and was written from the notes of Gill Taplin and Lynne Oldfield.

Development
of Consciousness:
Imitation,
Play and Learning

Forces Of Growth and Forces of Fantasy: Understanding the Dream Consciousness of the Young Child

Michaela Glöckler, MD

The Metamorphosis of Growth Forces into Forces of Fantasy and Imagination

We will look at two aspects of the developing etheric—the quality of the growth forces and the artistic forces. There is also a third aspect, which focuses on how these forces and qualities are raised into the consciousness of the child. To be conscious of these early growth forces, it is a help to go back in time to our own childhood and find the mood with which we viewed the world, its colors, smells, light, etc. What are our most beloved memories? Do they pertain to light and shadow, to the quality of early morning or of evening? Do they pertain to dreams? In dreams themselves, there is a big difference between the dreams of children and those of youngsters in puberty. If you can remember back to your own childhood, it is help towards meeting the children in the kindergarten.

When we look into the realm of life and the realm of thoughts, we see one aspect of both which is totally similar and the same. It is that there is a pure selflessness involved with both. What is life? We see living organisms such as plants growing, creatures crawling, jumping and leaping. We see human beings, ourselves, alive. If we ask the plant, "Who are you?" it would say, "I am a Cornell cherry." If I ask Susan, "Who are you?" she would say, "I am Susan." We experience life, but we do not focus on it. We are not conscious of it. Nobody would say, "I am a living being; I am alive."

It is the same with our thoughts. We do not focus on our thoughts, although we are proud of our intelligence. In *Philosophy of Spiritual Activity*, Rudolf Steiner describes thinking as the unconscious activity in our inner life. In this regard, the quality of life and of our thoughts is the same. They are of the same unconscious nature.

Regarding life, it is characterized by the fact that all the parts fit together into a whole. One cannot understand an isolated function of an organism or the working of a single isolated organ. It derives meaning only in relation to the whole. Life is a power of integration. An animal's stomach sitting on a dissecting table is not alive and can only reveal the secrets of its physical form. It is only when it is functioning within the animal that we can fully understand its living nature. We can say that the whole is much more than the sum of its many parts. If one part is disturbed, then the whole is disturbed.

It is the same when we look at our thoughts. There is a weaving together of concepts, words and descriptions to form a picture. If we look at a plant, for instance, we focus on the petals, the colors, the leaves, etc. The way they all come together makes the plant. It is the same with our thoughts. We cannot think one thought alone. If we think "small," for instance, we must think of something yet smaller and something bigger. Otherwise "small" has no meaning. We must see the relationships. In this way thoughts, too, do not live in isolation. They are part of a whole. The forces of life and thought are the unobserved selfless forces that are at work within us.

Here is a diagram of the growth and decline of physical forces.

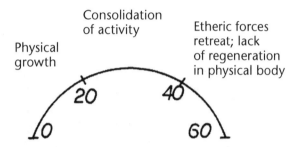

From the etheric point of view, things are very different than from the physical. Between forty and sixty years of age, the physical forces are more and more on their own while the etheric forces retreat. They are not available for the vitality and regeneration of the physical body. Where do the etheric forces go as they retreat from the physical in the older human being? They transform themselves into thoughts.

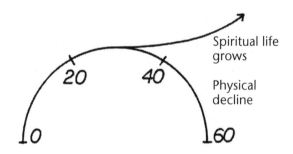

During its early years, the child is thinking with its growth forces. The whole way the child thinks is connected with growing up. In this first part of life, the etheric forces serve us by building up a healthy body. In this there is a natural egoism, as we put our etheric forces to use for ourselves. We focus on our own needs, and that

is natural in this first stage of life that lasts until age twenty.

In the second part of life, from twenty to forty, there is a change towards a selfless attitude in which we think more of others and encourage others. One sees mothers, teachers and others who begin around age forty or fifty to look outwardly at others. They become more objective and make good advisors. Others remain more egotistic, and this can develop destructively and can even become pathological. They are not growing old in a natural way, for the older person has the possibility of giving away, of doing without. This attitude is an inner dynamic of how the person thinks. The older person can forget self and think of others.

The etheric helps bring a balance between the individual and the society as well as between the parts of the cosmos. For example, there is a deep relationship between the plant and the sun though they are far away from each other. The plant is like an organ of the sun and earth together. This is like the mystery of life. All the plants and animals and earth together are an organism. We, too, are part of this living whole, and when we breathe in and out, we are participating in all that is around us.

Our thoughts, too, can connect with things very far away, like the plant relating to the sun. We can think of how the farthest stars behave. We can think of the hierarchies and of how they built up the cosmos. We can think of the laws of mathematics and of higher sciences. Our thoughts can penetrate all.

There is a moment, at around age three when the child says "I" to itself. Then the life of thought comes along. There was a three-year-old boy named Simeon who could not yet say "I." One of his aunts said, "Oh, he can't pronounce 's' properly. If he could, he would be able to say 'I.'" Simeon heard this and grew angry and said, "Why does she say that? Simeon can say 'I.'" After this he did not say "I" again until three weeks later when he painted a fiery picture, and someone asked who had painted it. He replied, "I did. I, I." After this he again forgot to say "I." Over the next three weeks it came and went. He displayed a tender awakening of the I. This is a word that cannot be learned. Even if he says, "Simeon can say I," he is not realizing it. He is only repeating it. It requires an awakening, a tender awakening of listening to the sounds of the soul, which lives more and more inside the being. It requires realizing the reality, and then one day, the thought is there.

Thoughts stand in relation to others and take meaning from others. There are situations in which a piece of chalk is of great worth, worth more than thousands of dollars, because in a particular context it is so necessary. We can never say that one of us or one of our thoughts is more important than another. Each has importance in relationship to the others.

In a child, the physical body is growing, and nearly all of the life forces are directed inward for the growth and regeneration of the physical. Very little is freed for thinking and that occurs only gradually in the early years. Around age six or seven, more of the life forces are freed, and then thinking activity can begin. In the older person, we have the opposite picture. There is very little that is directed towards rebuilding the physical, and most of the forces are available to be engaged in spiritual activity.

The etheric
is freed
for thinking

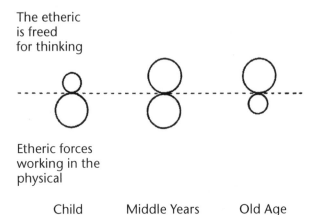

Etheric forces
working in the
physical

    Child   Middle Years   Old Age

We can see the etheric forces in life totally focusing on our constitution. In a good-natured sense they are egotistic. The immune system is the purest expression of the ego-activity on the etheric level. (It represents our "biological individuality.") The etheric forces serve our ego so the ego can be built up. It fights against the outside world to keep outside substances such as wrong blood or allergens from entering. The immune system is fighting off the world to serve the ego, to strengthen it.

The lemniscate is the picture of the etheric going through the mid-point of transformation and moving towards the outside. It goes around again and reenters the inside. The center or crossing point of the lemniscate is the point of metamorphosis. The growth forces go through that point and turn into something totally different, that is, they metamorphose into thinking forces. The growth forces, which turned inward, are now thinking forces, which turn outward.

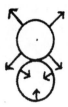

The life of thoughts makes sense only when it is turned outward in understanding the world, when it is oriented towards the outside. If we think too much of self, we become ill. There is a mystery of how to keep the physical body healthy, which has to do with the life of thought. If during the day, our thoughts go out into the world, then they may return to us at night and help us build up our bodies. Normally we regenerate ourselves at night. However, if we think too much of ourselves during the day, directing our thoughts too much in on ourselves, then during sleep these thoughts can have a destructive effect on our physical body.

We all contain great wisdom within us, the wisdom of *Study of Man*. We have to bring this to clarity in our thinking life. When we come together at conferences with their lectures, discussions and workshops, it gives us an opportunity to bring our thoughts from the unconscious realm into the conscious realm. Together we can take a step forward.

Soul Development and Artistic Activity

We all have music within us. We each have two octaves in us and singers have three octaves. This is the music within us, but other art forms also live within us. We have the possibility of doing form drawing and other activities that bring into us the forms of the mineral world, the plant world and the animal world. They bring into us human forms as well as the forms of astronomy and the abstract forms. A whole world of form lives within us.

We also have speech with its many facets. What can we express in words? We can use language to express our feelings. Through listening, we can come to the musical quality of language, and we can enter into another person's feelings. We can also control the will through language. Teachers know this. They can utter one word and there is silence in the room.

To create in the worlds of music, form and speech is a most important part of our inner life, our soul activity. Where does it come from and what are its relationships to the physical body? How are physical activities and soul activities related?

Leonardo da Vinci is well known as the painter of "The Last Supper." Rudolf Steiner often speaks of this painting and says if someone from the planet Mars were to come and look at "The Last Supper," he would intuitively understand the path of human earthly development. Art can speak of the deepest qualities of inner development, and this painting has particularly captured this. Although Leonardo was an engineer and was also well versed in medicine, he wrote a book to introduce painters to the art of painting. There is a passage in it on how the painter can control himself to become more and more an artist and less and less a beginning painter. The difference he points to is that the inexperienced painter always reproduces himself in his paintings; the more experienced painter is able to bring the being of the world into art.

The beginning painter is allowing the soul to express itself and what the soul is accustomed to, is building up the body. In the body, the soul is reproducing itself. This is what it is used to doing, and it continues to do so in the activity of painting. It is natural, then, that the inexperienced painter gives expression to this and, in a sense, reproduces himself on canvas. In a therapeutic situation, one sees the ill person reproducing himself in painting. It can be helpful to let him do this a time or two for diagnostic purposes, but to allow it to go on is unhealthy, for it can reinforce the illness.

The experienced artist moves beyond this wish to reproduce himself. He wants to bring the being of the world, of God, of nature into art. The experienced artist wants to reach this being and allow it to enter his art. Leonardo could reach the being of Christ and reveal it, its language, its inmost content, through his art. That is why a person from another planet could understand so much about human development on earth by gazing upon "The Last Supper." To paint in such a way requires a sacrifice, a movement away from self-expression and towards the expression of something higher. Such painting is a prayer to God to be allowed to bring something higher into the world through art.

Which laws live in the arts? Life began with whole activity; life arose from life. There was no hen or egg in the beginning. They were all together, for life is complex. It is a living system and does not arise from one little element or part. Physical laws deal with physical aspects; physical science pulls things apart. There are different laws that deal with the integrated whole, the composition. Rudolf Steiner says integration-activity comes out of the artistic realm.

If I pull some blood out of my veins, for example, and think this is the same as the blood in my body, this would be an illusion. Immediately it begins to deteriorate or break down. After two hours, the whole blood constitution is altered. Yet, it is a physical substance and each piece can be analyzed. All factions of the blood can be separated, and you can distinguish different substances. Physical research does this all of the time, but the secret of life is synthesis. Rudolf Steiner discovered this great secret of life, that life is integrative and synthesizing. All parts relate to one another. They are working to create a whole.

Laws of composition are integratively at work within us. The whole body is a composition itself. All of the arts live within us in slightly different ways. Music does not live in us in the same way as do painting or modeling. If you model or paint, you do not try to leave spaces between the colors or the forms, but one does leave spaces in music. Music lives in discontinuity, in the spaces or intervals between the notes. There is something living between the notes. That is an important aspect of music, and, in addition, music lives in time rather than in space. Also, music lives in the tension between two partners. We take the string of the monochord, which is drawn taut, and divide it into intervals. Without the tension, there could be no musical sound. Music lives in harmony and disharmony, tension and release of tension.

Where do we find something similar in the human being's constitution? Where do we find the spaces and the ability to make proportions as we do in music? In regard to spaces, consider the hand with its fingers spread apart. There is nothing between the fingers, and for this reason we can be so active with our hands. In the embryo, the hand begins by being filled in with a web-like substance. Then the fingers emerge and the

webbing retracts. There is a free space and the "music" enters. If this does not occur, then we must do surgery to free the fingers.

When we look for proportion in the human body, we can begin with the interval of the fifth. In the fifth, there is a beautiful proportion of 2:3. We see this in the physiology of the human being as well. On the right side of the chest the lung has three parts, while on the left only two. There is a breathing mood in the body itself of 2:3. In music, this is known as the fifth. We could look at other mathematical relationships in the body, for the whole body could be expressed in numbers—two eyes, two ears, etc. The whole nerve-sense system can be described in 1:2 relationships.

Another mathematical example from the body is the angle of the heart. The middle axis of the heart lies at an angle to the central axis of the body. On average, the angle the two make is 23 ½ degrees. This is the same angle as the earth to the sun on the ecliptic. There is no one detail of the body that is not full of sense and order and integrated into the laws of numbers, proportions and music. The world of music lies throughout our bodies.

Now let us consider the growth of the human being in the first twenty-one years.

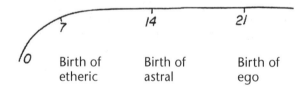

Every seven years during this period, we experience the birth of a body. What does this mean? What are these bodies for? The physical birth means the physical body is free to live in the physical world itself. The body moves and lives independently in the physical world. The birth of the etheric means the etheric is free in the etheric world. We see this moment of birth when the child starts to live in abstract memory. Before the independent life of the etheric, abstract memory is not possible. For instance, we can see a marionette play one day, and then again the following day. As adults we might think, "Now we know the play, wouldn't it be nice to have it a little different, to see different variations of it tomorrow?" We might counteract this tendency by telling ourselves that it is good to repeat things and take this on as an exercise. But for a young child, this is altogether different. The child knows it and knows it not. It knows it in repetition, and this continues until abstract memory is established. Abstract memory begins between the ages of six and eight.

In each birth, we experience that a force is freed to live in a new world. When the astral body is born around age fourteen, the world of feeling is born and can function in the astral world. Around twenty-one, the ego is born. This is the world of inner being, and we can now meet as inner being to inner being. Before this birth we could meet the astral, etheric or physical being of another. Now we can know one another at a deeper level. We can come to the center of the being and make contact there.

If we ask ourselves which forces deliver these birth moments of the soul, then we see that each body is revealing itself in its own realm. All gestures of the soul express their intentions in the body. The body reveals all of our feelings, thoughts and will. They all fit together into the laws of composition, and these are the same as the laws of art. We need years to study the laws of music, to realize that the laws of music are the laws of the astral body and of a very complicated emotional life. Likewise, we can study the laws of speech and comprehend the laws of the ego, the laws of painting and the laws of the etheric, and the laws of modeling and the laws of the physical.

Let us consider the laws of the ego. If a child is crying and moving around a great deal, and we cannot find any reason, then we have the feel-

ing that the child is moving without ego forces in a hyperkinetic way. When the child is really present, it acts in a different way. Likewise, if we drink too much alcohol, the ego withdraws and we have too little balance, for the ego power is the power of balance. Then we stumble about. When the ego is present, we can say, "I am," and this can be the dominating force in us. We can send "I am" and "I will" into every thought. Then we do only what we want, what we have directed ourselves to do. We identify with all that we do which is typical of this kind of ego power.

The art of speech represents this most beautifully, for it integrates the musical and sculptural laws. All of the physical laws are there, and we see them at work in the way we model our consonants with tongue, teeth, etc. The laws of the astral are there in the music of the language. Every language has its own music. The vowels live purely in this music, and you therefore cannot model vowels. They won't sound forth. Speech brings music and modeling into harmony. In speech, we bring the astral and the physical bodies together. The integrative power of the ego is the power of the word. After twenty-one, when the ego is there, we can consciously speak and say, "Yes, I want this," or "No, I don't want that." Until the time of maturity, we cannot consciously speak in this way.

Between fourteen and twenty-one, between puberty and maturity, the body changes considerably. During these years, the body finds a whole new harmony. In adolescence, around fifteen and sixteen, there is still a great deal of disharmony. The teenager looks at himself and has the feeling, "All the adults in the world look harmonious, only I don't." He looks at his thin chest and can't imagine how it will ever look normal. Then comes the last stretching of the chest, first crosswise and then from front to back. In adolescence, there are so many changes, but they do not all happen at once. They follow one another, giving the adolescent an awkward, unfinished look.

The adolescent's growth is discontinuous, not harmonious. It begins with the feet and moves upward. The poor eleven-year-old has such large feet. One has the feeling in looking at an adolescent that every part is growing for itself. It is as if each part is a separate tone, and we are unable to see the whole composition. All the tones are not yet there. The beard grows in patches, not all at once. The breasts mature unevenly, often growing one at a time. It is as if a conductor of an orchestra is calling forth one instrument after another. At the end, they are all called forth and playing together. The growth looks funny if we don't see the musical process at work.

These phenomena are not typical of the preschool years. The first period of growth is a very harmonious one. During the first nine years, there is holiness present in the growth. The young child's physical development is normally harmonious, but their emotional life, their thinking and their will still need our care and attention. These are qualities not yet born in the child. Surrounding the child, there is an embryonic atmosphere. With which eyes am I allowed to behold this? To look at the unborn forces of the human being is like looking into the uterus of the soul. We must represent the ego forces of the child so that the growth is harmonious and good. We are part of the caring, ripening activity.

Consider our own soul activity in terms of music when we meet another person. If it is a person we like, we experience a major mood within us. We feel, "Oh, good, here comes a person who makes me happy." If another comes towards us, we may feel unhealthy, tense and drawn in. Why do we feel this dissonance? If I bring myself into a new position in relation to this person, then a new tone will arise, a tone that may bring the dissonance into harmony. Every tone needs two partners who function like the two fixed ends of the monochord. Without them there can be no tone. Never put the consequences of disharmony on the other person, lay-

ing guilt upon them. You are a partner, and the tension exists between the two of you, even as it exists between the two ends of the monochord.

In a marionette play, we have a beautiful composition of moving pictures, speech and music. If it were told with the mood of drama, then isolated emotions would awaken. That is not possible for the young child, for at this age, these developments of the inner life are still unborn. We do not want to awaken them. Young children need harmonious interactions.

The Developing Consciousness of the Child

In thinking back to our infancy and childhood, what were our thoughts and actions? I remember feeling awake in all parts of soul life as a child. I felt sorrow, hurt and delight. The young child already has an ego and emotions, but not in developed form. Around age twenty, the ego is born and can stand freely in the world, but all of the forces already exist in an unripened stage earlier in life.

When we try to form a picture of what is present and ready to be freely used in the young child, then we see that the child is totally there and present in the physical body and is fully awake in the senses. These can be used and developed in early childhood. Imitation is present at a young age and speaks to the senses. Activity is important in these years, because the physical body likes to move, be active and skillful, and adapt to the world. Children delight in being active from morning to evening. When they are being active, every hindrance hurts them, so to do what they like is a pure delight for children. These things exist in the life of the young child, while all else is still in development.

The young child experiences events differently than we do. As mature adults, we take things into our soul life. The young child cannot do this yet. If the young child has a problem or is shocked, he will often wet himself, the experience "runs out," whereas, we hold the experience in. If the child feels joy, she begins to jump up and down. The whole body wants to participate in the joyous experience. We don't usually display our joy with the whole body, except at a football game when we jump up and down. Then we can experience the game like a child, but, usually, if something fills us with joy, we smile or laugh. That is like a small jump.

Consider sense perception and how it relates to the soul realm. When we read the biographies of great people, such as Proust, and consider their experiences of childhood, we can see what intense sense impressions they had as children. A child experiences the atmosphere of a festival or vacation in a most intensive way. At age thirty, I returned to a beloved vacation spot of my childhood. I tried not to be sad, but my experience as an adult was so much paler than what I remembered from my childhood. The house was so small; the stall for the animals was not at all special. Even the flowers in the meadow, and the sky and water seemed rather "normal" and not of that glory which the child's memory put on it.

In childhood, the life of thoughts and the life of the senses are still a unity. They are not yet divided. Therefore, the experience of the senses is very intense. It is also why children can imitate and can understand immediately what is going on. They intuitively know when something is wrong. They can intuitively understand their sense experiences in the moment that they are occurring. As adults, we need to understand by thinking about the experience afterwards. Later, when abstract memory awakens, the child will be able to separate sense impressions from thinking. This is an important step, for in order to learn something, sense perceptions have to be separate from thinking.

The child's perception of the world is very different from those of the adult, for he sees thought life woven around and within its sur-roundings. He looks at a dark corner, for example, and sees the shadows move. He experiences the inner meaning of darkness. Something jumps out of the darkness, and the child is frightened. He runs to his mother who turns on the light and says there is nothing there. The child is often not understood at a deeper level, but he is consoled that the mother is strong enough to bring light into the darkness. The child has both these experiences; he is misunderstood and consoled at the same time.

We need to realize that every thought is a living reality for the child. She sees the flower and experiences the inner reality of the flower; she sees the being of the flower. The child experiences not only the outlook but also the "inlook," the inner being or "I Am" of the object perceived. The child is not awake like the adult is. She cannot separate the inner from the outer and think about the one or the other. She is neither fully awake, nor is she asleep. Her consciousness is in between, like a dream. Yet within that consciousness it is alert to the world and takes everything in.

Let us try to understand waking and sleeping more fully. What happens during sleep in the adult? The astral and ego leave the physical and etheric bodies behind and live in the realm of the Cosmos. The child with his unripened soul life does not sleep properly in this way. The astral and ego are too involved in the physical and etheric. To sleep in such a way that the astral and ego are free of the physical and etheric requires that the etheric body be born. This does not happen until age seven, but it takes a few more years for the freed etheric to be well established. After seven, the astral and ego can begin to come to the pure astral realm in sleep, then the thought life can switch off during sleep.

The child's consciousness occurs in stages. At the age of three, a new self-consciousness begins as the child experiences herself as an "I" separate from others. At nine, there is a crisis in the development as the child senses its "I" at a deeper level. A self-sensitivity exists, and the child feels, "I am alone, I am a personality." Before that, she has felt a part of her surroundings, however with a growing self-consciousness. Between eight and ten, she feels more fully apart. She feels separate from her mother and father and secretly thinks that they are not her true mother and father. Perhaps she asks, "Are you sure I am your child? You didn't mix me up with another at birth?"

Now the sleep life changes and the nightmares of the small child stop. The child begins to sleep more deeply. During these first nine years, the child awakens at night with fears and visions because the astral and ego are still so close. The child is half-awake at night and dreams in the elemental world. As adults, we move through this realm quickly, and if we are tired enough, we are not disturbed by it. The young child cannot sleep properly, but he also can't awaken properly. He is in between.

An awakened person can identify what things are good for it out of an awakened process of knowing the thing itself. A dreamy adult can intuit what is good and not good but can't explain it. The astral and ego are too closely bound to the physical and etheric in such a person. It takes courage to be awake as an adult, to develop an independent personality. Many people are fearful and don't want an awakened adult consciousness.

The dream consciousness of the child is easily misunderstood. A parent may say, "My child is interested in all of the world—technology, nature, et cetera. She is so awake to the world, she is not at all dreamy." But the young child does live deeply into the world around her. She lives through the senses and experiences all of the qualities of the world. She is not awake to think abstractly about the world as the adult is, but she is actively taking in the world through the senses coupled with thinking. In the nighttime, she is more awake than we are. In the daytime, she is more asleep than we.

How can we help the child during this stage? Rudolf Steiner says that before age nine, the most important thing is to help children to properly sleep. Since children are more awake than we are in the night, it can be a help to some children to have a night light on. This gives a certain day aspect at night so they don't feel too alone in sleepy awakeness.

The child is also helped to sleep at night if he has been helped to awaken properly in the day. This occurs through the purposeful activities that the adult does in the child's presence during the day. The child needs to experience clarity and purposeful direction in the daytime. Then he experiences proper calm at night.

There is a constant process of transforming the unconscious into the conscious. In the unconscious there is much wisdom. An awake adult can experience the conscious part of thought life through learning, but can't experience spontaneously the unconscious part of thoughts. The dreamy adult gets an intuition and spontaneously realizes something.

The child experiences wisdom, but not in an awake way. She can't judge, analyze or prove things. Instead, she has a capacity for fantasy, that is nothing other than experiencing a small part of this wisdom which is freed from the growth forces and is available as fantasy.

Conscious

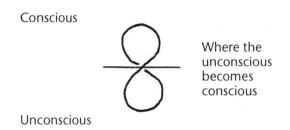

Where the unconscious becomes conscious

Unconscious

The child lives in the realm of pictures and wisdom, but he is mixed up totally with sense perception. In one stick he sees the whole world. With the stick and a piece of yarn, he can be a fisherman, a priest or so many other things. He is working with the world of growth forces which are gradually being freed and will reappear in the soul, first as fantasy forces and later as imagination and then as thinking forces.

All living things have a spiritual component. The elemental beings are the spiritual fundamentals of things and are thought realities. In all living things, there are also destructive forces. The dead is inborn in every living being; every cell contains within it an aspect of death. We might consider this to be a "bad" being, a destructive being, but we need destruction so that new life can be born. If nothing died, nothing could be born. A balance occurs between life giving forces and death giving forces. Only the human being is capable of going out of balance between these two polarities. Through our ego, we need to live in a balanced way, keeping life and death in harmony.

When the child learns to walk in the first year, she finds her first ego balance. In speech in the second year, she finds her social balance. In thought in the third year, she finds her spiritual balance. In finding its ego or I, she finds this spiritual balance, this balance in thought.

The whole development of the ego is part of a huge process of finding balance. If we continue to live more and more out of balance as we do today, with no balance between spiritual and physical activity, then it will not be possible for the earth and the human being to endure much longer. There is no god we can make responsible for this balance. We must look to ourselves for this.

There are many spiritual trainings that try to reactivate an old stage of dream consciousness, which we had as children. It is not difficult to move in this direction, for it lives in all of us. It is beautiful to be a child, and it is understandable that many adults prefer this and want to be more like children and not fully adult-like. As adults, we can achieve a new stage of awakeness and need not turn to methods that reactivate

the dream stage of childhood. Turning to drugs, alcohol, reliance on a guru or utilizing certain spiritual techniques leads us backwards rather than forwards.

We can give children a beautiful security of dream consciousness and gently guide them towards awakeness. We need not push them out too quickly, but guide them out. If they have not fully experienced the dream consciousness of early childhood, then as adults they turn back and seek this lost paradise. They seek the dream experience through drugs, for instance. We all had something similar to a drug experience in childhood when colors, pictures, et cetera, were so vivid, and we could fully live within them. Now we can find it in new ways as awakened persons.

Rudolf Steiner describes fantasy in this way: "The soul is able to withdraw a certain energy for other purposes, and this is the power of fantasy: the natural power of growth metamorphosed into a soul force." (*Understanding Young Children*, p. 75) For the child in the dream consciousness of fantasy, life is like being in a theater in which good thoughts appear like good elemental beings and bad thoughts appear as well because of the work of the destructive forces. These destructive forces are always there in nature, working in the processes of digestion, for example. They appear in the child with as much reality as an outer experience of the senses. They create a specific type of dream consciousness for the child.

In our times, the child's dream consciousness is strongly touched by the destructive forces, and fear arises. There is a very strong element of fear in children today. The child lives in the world of technology today, and every technological event is based on destruction. Electricity, for example, is created out of the earth's destruction. To remove oil or gas from the earth is always a process of destruction, even when we use it to construct something. We must always look to the balance of energy. If we use windmills, do we have a positive balance or a negative balance of destruction? Or if we sit in a room lit by a 100 watt light and do nothing, then perhaps it would be better to do nothing in the dark. Of course, we must use the forces of technology if it is for constructive purposes. If we use the washing machine, this uses much energy, which is destructive, but we can balance this by doing something worthwhile with the freed time. Finding this balance for the destructive elements of technology is one of the moral problems of our time. When the imbalance towards destructiveness is too great, then fear arises, a fear of the elemental beings of destruction. This happens when there is not a balance of constructive beings, and children are very sensitive to this imbalance. It makes them fearful.

During the last twenty years, for the first time in mankind, we are experiencing sleep problems in children under age seven. There is coldness present in the children. Sometimes it is physical and can be corrected, but often it exists in the awareness of destruction that brings fear to the children. Often they want to come into the parents' bed during the first nine years, and this can even be a help to the child. This can be a little cure, but the child should not be exposed to adult sexual activity, for this is too great an experience for them and can lead to other problems.

What children truly need is for the family to find the correct balance between constructive and destructive forces in the home. It is also of help for the religious life to arise in the home that can bring balance to all processes, which seem senseless if not understood in the light of inner understanding.

Dr. Michaela Glöckler is currently the head of the Medical Section at the Goetheanum in Dornach, Switzerland. She has been active as a pediatrician and school doctor in Germany and is the author of A Guide to Child Health, *Floris Books. This article is a summary of three lectures recorded by Nancy Foster and Joan Almon and reviewed by Dr. Glöckler.*

The Vital Role of Play in Early Childhood Education

Joan Almon

The ability to play is one of the principal criteria of mental health. —Ashley Montagu

The Universal Nature of Play

In over 30 years of working with young children, families, and teachers in Waldorf kindergartens all over the world, I have observed one consistent feature of childhood: *creative play is a central activity in the lives of healthy children.* Play helps children weave together all the elements of life as they experience it. It is an outlet for the fullness of their creativity, and it is an absolutely critical part of their childhood. The unique qualities of each child become apparent in the way they play. Some cultural differences emerge, for children imitate what they see around them and play it out. But there are strong universal qualities in play. For example, three-year-olds around the world play in similar ways; their play is different from that of five- or six-year-olds.

The universal nature of play is evident. One can speak of the language of play that unites young children all over the world. It is fascinating to watch children from different countries playing together. Although they may not be able to speak one word of the other's language, they can play together for hours. They enter a common realm where the external differences of language and culture are small compared to the vast similarities embedded in the child's inner urge to play.

Although play is a steady part of healthy children's lives, it is not easy to define what play is. I prefer to think of it as a bubbling spring of health and creativity within each child—and, for that matter, within every human being. Sometimes this spring seems to stop flowing, but it remains at the heart of every human being and, with a bit of effort, the blockages can be cleared away and a creative, playful spirit can flow again. This can happen at any age.

When young children are ill, they often stop playing for a few days. As soon as they are better, their parents notice the spark of play shining in their eyes again. In general, when children are able to play creatively, they blossom and flourish. If they stop playing over an extended period of time, they can suffer a decline and even become depressed or show signs of other illnesses.

Play is of central importance in a child's life. This is well supported by decades of research, some of which is described in this article.

Despite its central importance in children's healthy development, play—in the creative, open-ended sense in which I use the term—is now seriously endangered in the United States and many other countries. It is being pushed out of children's lives for a number of reasons. I will mention four:

1. Children have become dependent on electronic entertainment: television, videos, and computers. U.S. children spend three to five hours per day in front of screens outside of school hours. This leaves little time or inclination for real play. When media-filled children do play, it is naturally full of media characters and stories. It becomes increasingly hard for children to make up their own creative stories in play, for their imaginations have been overpowered by what they have seen on the screen. In extreme cases, children are fixated on these screen images and will not allow any changes in the story they are playing out.

2. Kindergarten programs in the U.S. focus so strongly on teaching literacy, numeracy, and other academic subjects that many children no longer have time to play in kindergarten. Many kindergartens are now full-day. In a typical six-hour public kindergarten in the New York or Washington area, for instance, children spend ninety minutes per day on early literacy drills, sixty minutes on mathematics, and thirty minutes on science. They have about thirty minutes for outdoor play but no time for indoor play. They have music once a week, art once a week, and a few other subjects. In Montgomery County, Maryland, near Washington, D.C., I have been told that the word "play" does not appear at all in the kindergarten curriculum.

3. This academic approach to early learning is shifting downward. Three- and four-year-olds are now expected to engage in far more early writing and reading activities than ever before. Head Start, the U.S. federal program for low-income children, was forced to revise its curriculum this year to make more time for early literacy and less time for play. Children will be assessed on their overall gains and programs will be evaluated according to how the children do. Since it is difficult, although not impossible, to assess children on how well they play, normal assessments focus on how many letters and numbers children know, and how many of the basic steps in literacy and numeracy they have taken.

4. The amount of time spent in sports and other organized activities for young children has increased greatly in the past thirty years, beginning with pre-schoolers, so that children have little time for their own play activities.

Dr. Alvin Rosenfeld, a noted child and adolescent psychiatrist who is concerned about the demise of play and of family time, recently quoted these statistics:

This over-scheduled family style has insinuated itself into the fabric of our family lives. In the past twenty years, structured sports time has doubled, unstructured children's activities have declined by 50%, household conversations have become far less frequent, family dinners have declined 33%, and family vacations have decreased by 28% (Rosenfeld, 2004).

Given the importance of play for children's physical, social, emotional, and mental development, the demise of play will certainly have serious consequences during childhood and throughout children's lives. Indeed, there is growing concern about what kind of society we are creating if a generation of children grow up without play and the creative thinking that emerges from play. Can democracy survive if creative thinking dies out?

I have observed the steady decline of play over the past thirty years, but even I was astonished by a recent call from a counselor in an elementary school near Washington. She had been talking with a first-grade class and used the word "imagination." When they stared blankly at her, she explained its meaning, but the children continued to look puzzled. She gave an example from her own childhood when she loved to play Wonder Woman. She would put on a cape, she said, and run down the hill near her house with arms outstretched, pretending to be aloft. "That's imagination, when you pretend to be someone you're not," she explained to the children.

"But we don't know how to do that," said one child, and all the others nodded their heads in agreement. Not one child in that first grade seemed to know what imaginative play was.

What Research Tells Us about Play

There has been a great deal of research about play over many decades. In general, the research shows strong links between creative play and language, physical, cognitive, and social development. According to researcher Sara Smilansky, children who show the greatest capacities for social make-believe play also display more imagination and less aggression, and a greater ability to use language for speaking and understanding others (Smilansky, p. 35).

Research in Germany in the 1970s showed that by fourth grade children who had attended play-oriented kindergartens surpassed those from academic-oriented kindergartens in physical, social, emotional, and mental development. The findings were so compelling that Germany switched all its kindergartens back to being play-oriented (*Der Spiegel*, pp. 89-90).

In the U.S., the research of the High/Scope Foundation in Ypsilanti, Michigan is often cited. There, sixty-nine low-income children, ages three and four, who were considered to be at risk of future school failure were divided into three groups. One, called the High/Scope group, was offered a program with much child-initiated activity, including play. Another, called the Direct Instruction group, received much instruction in academic subjects. The third, called the Nursery Program, was a combination of the other two. As the children grew up, those who had been in the High/Scope and Nursery programs succeeded in school and life significantly better than the children in the more academic, Direct Instruction program. At age fifteen, the following results were noted:

Initially, all three curriculum approaches improved young children s intellectual performance substantially, with the average IQs of children in all three groups rising twenty-seven points. By age fifteen, however, students in the High/ Scope group and the Nursery School group. . . reported only half as much delinquent activity as the students in the Direct Instruction group. . . (High/Scope).

By the time the children had grown up and were age twenty-three, the research continued to point to a much higher success level for those who had been able to play in nursery school. The High/Scope and Nursery School groups showed gains over the Direct Instruction group on seventeen different variables. At a time when young people in the U.S. are going to prison in record numbers, I think it is especially important to note that the Direct Instruction group had significantly more felony arrests than the other two groups. They also had had more years of special education for emotional impairment, and their level of schooling did not rise as high as the youngsters from the High/Scope group.

A recent study by Rebecca Marcon of the University of North Florida found results similar to those of High/Scope when children from different preschool programs were followed through fourth grade. Those who had attended play-oriented programs where child-initiated activities predominated did better academically than those who had attended academic-oriented programs (Marcon).

I would have thought that such research alone would convince educators, parents and policymakers that it is foolish—and even dangerously unhealthy—to immerse three- and four-year-olds in direct instruction programs. Yet these programs are gaining favor throughout the United States. The President and Congress have set the highest levels ever for academic achievement for Head Start children, and have supported legislation that would influence all pre-school programs to move in this direction.

Recent research looks at how young children learn in terms of brain development. This new research does not seem to produce radical new findings about play and learning. Rather, it confirms that the healthy essentials of childhood, including forming trusting relations with caring adults and exploring the world through play, movement, language, and hands-on activities, are in fact essential.

Brain researchers continually remind us that the brain is not an isolated organ in the body. It is linked to everything else—to language, to movement, to social and emotional experiences. Thus, when the hands, the eyes, the ears, or the heart are being stimulated through life activity, so is the brain.

Dr. Frank Wilson, a neurologist at Stanford University who has specialized in working with performing artists with hand problems, makes the point that an unusually large part of the brain is linked to the human hand. Thus, if you want to stimulate the brain, get children involved in hands-on activities. He is concerned that children today use their hands primarily for computer operations. He does not consider this to be true hands-on learning and is concerned that the brain is actually under-stimulated in ways that really count. Wilson says, "I would argue that any theory of human intelligence which ignores the interdependence of hand and brain function, the historic origins of that relationship, or the impact of that history on developmental dynamics in modern humans, is grossly misleading and sterile" (Wilson, p. 7).

Jane Healy, a learning expert who has written extensively about brain development and about computer use in childhood, emphasizes the need for children to move their bodies and to be engaged in nature and in life. At birth the brain has the capacity to learn to walk, run, jump, and

do a host of other things. But the capacity in the brain develops only if the child actually *does* these things and doesn't just watch them being done on a screen. The brain is waiting to be awakened, but it needs a multi-sensory, enriched environment to be awakened (Healy, p. 177).

It is important to note here that an enriched environment does not mean an over-stimulating environment. It means a normally enriched environment. My experience is that children thrive when given space for indoor and outdoor play and have a sense of comfort from knowing that a caring adult is nearby, preferably doing things like gardening, woodwork, cooking, or cleaning. These life activities stimulate children's play. Add some basic play materials like logs, stones, cloths, and ropes, from which they can fashion their own toys, plus some artistic materials for self-expression, and a healthy scattering of stories, songs, and verses, and you quickly have a playful child.

Under-stimulation, such as I have seen in very poor kindergartens in Africa, is a problem, but so is over-stimulation, which I see in nearly every kindergarten in the United States. Children need a calm and lovely environment, full of warm-hearted human beings who create a sense of security, are engaged in meaningful activity, and provide children with a reasonable amount of materials that can be used in dozens of different ways.

Some research shows a direct link between play and the development of mathematical abilities. Ranald Jarrell of the University of Arizona reports that "play is vital to the development of children's mathematical thinking. Unlike some forms of knowledge, mathematical knowledge, which deals with the relationships between and among things, cannot be learned by hearing adults talk about it. Experimental research on play shows a strong relationship between play, the growth of mathematical understanding, and improved mathematical performance" (Hirsh-Pasek and Golinkoff, p. 220).

As mentioned above, Sara Smilansky found strong evidence that the children who were best able to engage in sociodramatic play, that is, who could play with others in make-believe activities, also showed the greatest gains in many forms of language and social development. She also found that the more advanced players developed more imagination and were less aggressive (Klugman and Smilansky, p. 35).

The development of problem-solving skills has also been linked to play. One type of these skills is called "convergent," where there is one solution to a problem. The other is "divergent," where there are many possible ways to solve a problem. Both are needed in life. The former is what is measured on most standardized tests, which have a single correct answer to a question. Increasingly, it is the type of thinking we educate children for. But the second type is what is often called for by life. Complex social, political, or economic questions rarely have just one clear-cut answer.

In *Einstein Never Used Flash Cards*, the authors report on a simple but impressive piece of research. One group of three-year-olds, led by a child named Amala, was given convergent materials to play with, including puzzles and other toys that have just one right way to be used. Michael's group was given blocks and other divergent play materials that can be used in many ways. Then both groups were asked to build a village with forty-five pieces of the play materials that Michael's group had been using.

Researchers watched both groups to see how many structures they built and how many names they created for their structures. Michael's group built more structures and had more diverse names for them. When they had problems with the task, they did not give up but found new solutions. They used trial and error a lot.

"Amala's group acted very differently," the authors write. "Having played with convergent toys they had one right answer, they got stuck and did the same things over and over again when they couldn't do a divergent problem. They also gave up more quickly than Michael's group. It was as if they had learned that problems have a single answer. . . " The authors go on to point out that school generally teaches children to answer questions correctly. But play teaches children to think "outside the box." If one wants children to grow up with creative capacities, then play is essential. "Where does creativity come from?" ask the authors. "From play—good old unmonitored, unstructured free and open play" (Hirsh-Pasek and Golinkoff, pp. 223-224).

A similar link between play and creativity in adulthood was researched by Stuart Brown, a psychiatrist then working in Texas. He interviewed prisoners who were incarcerated for murder or very aggressive driving that had resulted in a death and found that these prisoners did not have a history of play in their lives. In contrast, when he interviewed winners of the MacArthur "genius" award, a prestigious prize given to creative individuals in a wide range of fields by the John D. and Catherine T. MacArthur Foundation, he found that nearly all had a rich history of play from childhood onwards.

In all, Brown interviewed about 8,000 people. What they told him confirmed his conclusion that healthy, varied play in childhood is necessary "for the development of empathy, social altruism and . . . a repertoire of social behaviors enabling the player to handle stress. It fosters curiosity, is a major catalyst to learning, and through long acquaintance with playful imagination, gives angry provoked individuals alternatives to acting impulsively and violently" (Stuart Brown, web site).

Animal Research Linking Play and Brain Development

A number of researchers have looked at the relationship between play and brain size. John Byers of the University of Idaho compared the playful wombats with the more docile koala bears and found that the wombats had bigger brains per body weight. When he and other researchers tracked the actual rates of brain growth from infancy to maturity in different animal types, they found correlations between periods of rapid brain growth and periods of more active play (cited in Furlow, 2001).

There is no certainty yet as to why play and brain size may go together. One explanation is that the most active periods of play may correlate with times when more synapses are forming in the brain. Synapses are the connections that develop between neighboring neurons. Another explanation is that play may stimulate the development of myelin, a fatty substance that allows nerves to transmit more complex information than they can while uncoated.

Researchers tend to be cautious in their conclusions and so also point out that perhaps there is not a direct correlation between play and brain growth. Both might be stimulated by another factor such as metabolism. More research is needed, but meanwhile there is a growing sense that play and brain growth are in fact related.

Marc Bekoff of the University of Colorado studied coyote pups at play. He found that their behavior was much more varied and unpredictable than that of adults. He reasons that acting in this way activates many parts of the brain and that their brains receive a great deal of stimulation from their playful behavior. Bekoff concludes that "play creates a brain that has greater behavioral flexibility and improved potential for learning later in life." He also states that "people have not paid enough attention to the amount of the brain activated by play." He adds that there is enormous cognitive development in play (cited in Furlow).

The Relationship of Play to Health

As an early childhood teacher, I was struck by how often parents said things like this to me: "My child was sick, but it wasn't too serious. He played the whole time." Or they might say, "She was really sick and didn't play at all." Unconsciously, they were associating play with health. There is a great wisdom in this.

The relationship was confirmed for me by the psychiatrist Stuart Brown. As a young intern he worked with very ill children in hospitals where one often did not know if the children would live or die. He noticed that sometimes he would enter the room of a very sick child, but the child would have a playful gleam in his or her eye for the first time. He found consistently that this was an indication of a return to health (Brown, State of World Forum).

Many other experts on play also point to the relationship between children's overall health and their ability to play. Marc Bekoff of the University of Colorado says play is a sign of healthy development. He adds, "When play drops out, something is wrong." He adds that we have become a "play-less society" and points to problems such as the prevalence of organized sports rather than spontaneous play and the fact that school is beginning earlier and is becoming increasingly exam-oriented. If these trends continue, there is even less likelihood that children will be given time to play in the future (cited in Furlow, 2001).

Bryant Furlow, writing in *New Scientist*, expresses concern about the relationship between play and mental health: "Children destined to suffer mental illnesses such as schizophrenia as adults, for example, engage in precious little social play early in life. But can a lack of play affect the creativity and learning abilities of normal children?" No one knows for sure, but there is a growing concern that play is disappearing from childhood and that this will affect children's physical, social, and emotional health. Furlow points out that when "rat pups are denied the opportunity to play [they] grow smaller neocortices and lose the ability to apply social rules when they do interact with their peers" (Furlow, 2001).

Implications for the Future

If imaginative free play continues to disappear from childhood, I anticipate several serious outcomes:

- An increase in mental illness beginning in childhood.

- Difficulties in the way children socialize and communicate with each other, including more aggression in social relationships.

- A change in the development of thinking with a loss of divergent thinking and a growing emphasis on convergent thinking.

Already there is serious concern about increases in mental illness in childhood, including depression, hyperactive disorders, and anxiety disorders. The World Health Organization of the United Nations reports that by the year 2020 childhood neuropsychiatric disorders will rise proportionately by over 50 percent, internationally, to become one of the five most common causes of morbidity, mortality, and disability among children (Surgeon General, 2001).

There is also a growing concern among teachers, psychologists, and others that children's social capacities are weakening. In general, technologically developed countries place such an emphasis on intellectual achievement that they forget how critical social abilities are. We are now seeing extreme situations, the cause of which is not yet known, such as the increase in Asperger syndrome and other forms of autism. The state of California reported a 210 percent increase in autism between 1987 and 1998, and the median age of patients dropped from fifteen to nine years (California Department of Developmental Services, p. 10). Many feel that the increase in autism may be emblematic of a more widespread problem—the growth of a social type of autism caused by too many hours staring at screens instead of interacting with humans in play and other ways, as well as other factors. This situation is not yet documented and needs research.

The example of Amala and Michael above showed how creative play is linked to open-ended divergent thinking. If one does not develop this type of exploratory, open-ended thinking, how does one approach today's social, political, economic, and ecological problems? Not many of our complex contemporary issues can be solved with a simple right or wrong answer. Most are far more intricate and require trial and error and a willingness to keep going through difficulties until one comes to the best solution possible. I am very concerned that without opportunities for open-ended, imaginative play, our children will not be capable of this type of creative thinking as they grow older. Modern democratic processes call for complex divergent thinking, and without it the tendency to favor authoritarian decision-making, where one person says what is right or wrong, grows much greater. We may well become a society with a narrow orientation to problem solving. When situations are not easily resolved, we may become more inclined to resort to aggression and violence, rather than complex problem solving.

I cannot help but wonder whether the politicians who are pushing for early literacy and other forms of direct instruction for three- to six-year-olds are simply ignorant of the importance of play, or whether they would prefer a populace whose creative thinking and social capacities are impaired. Such a populace would find it harder to participate in a diverse, democratic society, and might well opt to be ruled by a government with a strong hand.

Restoring Play

There are many steps that can be taken to restore play to children's lives, but here are a few:

1. Leading educators, health professionals, and other child advocates need to work together to examine the role of play in childhood and the ways in which it is endangered. Their findings need to be publicized as widely as possible, with an emphasis on what children need for healthy development.

The formation of commissions of prominent experts needs to be done as quickly as possible, for there are many countries at this time that are on the brink of eliminating play in early childhood education in favor of direct instruction of academic subjects for young children. The experience in the United States is that once this change happens, it is very difficult to reverse the process. The U.S. has offered academic instruction to five-year-olds in kindergartens for thirty years. There is no evidence that it has worked, and there is much concern that it has caused great harm. Nonetheless, rather than admitting failure, policymakers are now insisting that one start teaching reading through direct instruction to three- and four-year-olds. They believe that the younger one begins the better, despite research and experience that prove the opposite.

In 2002, the U.S. Senate's Health, Education, Labor and Pensions Committee prepared legislation to support preschool programs for three- and four-year-olds. Such financial support is badly needed, but the legislation was controversial. In part, it called for healthy steps toward a holistic approach to early childhood education, but it also repeatedly called for early literacy and offered bonuses to states that could show gains in "kindergarten readiness." These gains would almost certainly need to be shown in academic areas, as few programs assess children's gains in social and emotional development. The Alliance for Childhood issued a statement of concern that was signed by leading educators and health professionals and was distributed in the Senate and to other government officials (Alliance for Childhood).

2. Parents, educators, and health professionals need to become activists on behalf of young children and engage directly in the development of healthy approaches to early childhood education.

At present, in the United States and other countries, politicians have actively entered the realm of early childhood education and are insisting that early childhood programs promote early literacy and numeracy at the expense of child-initiated activity. This needs to be countered by grassroots and other forms of activism in every community and in every preschool and kindergarten program. Research and experience clearly show what young children actually need for balanced, healthy development. It is time that the fruits of that research and experience are implemented in every early childhood setting. To do anything else is to promote the miseducation of children.

3. Develop large-scale public education campaigns to help parents and professionals understand the importance of play and how to strengthen children's play.

Most early childhood teachers in the U.S., for instance, receive little or no training in helping children play. Since the play patterns of children are already disturbed, simply encouraging children to play is often not enough. Teachers and parents need workshops, literature, videos, and other educational tools to help them support children in play.

4. Parents and community leaders need to work together to create safe play spaces for children.

Children need play spaces where they can run in the grass, roll down hills, and, if possible, play in a stream or fountain. Such play spaces need some adult supervision at a paid or volunteer level. Just as parents now volunteer to coach sports, they can be encouraged to volunteer to supervise free play spaces and receive training on how to do this. A starting place is to organize a play day in a neighborhood or community (International Play Association).

Conclusion

Research and experience show strong relationships between a child's capacity to play and his or her overall development—physical, social, emotional, and intellectual. There is reason to be deeply concerned that as play disappears from childhood, children will suffer in all these areas. In many countries, play is diminishing and the first indications of such suffering are becoming apparent. Yet nation after nation is rushing toward removing play from young children's lives in the misguided belief that three- to six-year-olds are ripe and ready for direct instruction in early literacy and other academic subjects. For the sake of the children, and for the sake of the society they are part of, this direction needs to be reversed now and play needs to be restored as a healthy essential of childhood.

(Parts of this article are adapted from one that appeared in the book All Work and No Play, *Sharna Olfman, editor, Praeger, 2003.)*

Bibliography

Alliance for Childhood. "Children from birth to five: A statement of first principles on early education for educators and policymakers." Retrieved 1.29.03 from http://allianceforchildhood.com/projects/play/index.htm

Brown, Stuart. State of the World Forum, Whole Child Roundtable, San Francisco, 1999.

Brown, Stuart. "About us: Stuart Brown, Founder of the Institute for Play." Retrieved 3.14.04 from http://www.instituteforplay.com/13stuart_brown.htm

California Department of Developmental Services. Changes in the population of persons with autism and PDD's in California's developmental services system: 1987-1998. A report to the legislature, 1999. Retrieved 1.29.03 from http://www.dds.cahwnet.gov/autism/pdf/autism_report_1999.pdf

Der Spiegel. German news magazine, No. 20, 1977.

Furlow, Bryant. "Play's the Thing," *New Scientist*, No. 2294, p. 28, 2001; http://archive.newscientist.com/secure/article/article.jsp?rp=1&id=mg17022944.600.

Healy, Jane. *Failure to Connect.* New York: Simon and Schuster, 1998.

High/Scope Summary. "Different effects from different preschool models: High/Scope preschool curriculum comparison study." Drawn from works by Schweinhart, L. J., & Weikart, D. P., et. al. Retrieved 1.29.03 from http://www.highscope.org/Research/curriccomp.htm

Hirsh-Pasek, Kathy and Roberta Michnik Golinkoff. *Einstein Never Used Flash Cards.* Rodale, 2003.

International Play Association, USA. "What is a Playday?" Retrieved 3.10.04 from http://www.ipausa.org/playday.htm

Marcon, Rebecca A. Moving up the grades: Relationship between preschool model and later school success. *Early Childhood Research and Practice*, 4, (1), [Electronic Version], Spring, 2002.

Montagu, Ashley. *Growing Young.* New York: McGraw-Hill, 1981.

Olfman, Sharna. *All Work and No Play: How educational reforms are harming our preschoolers.* Westport, CT: Praeger, 2003.

Rosenfeld, Alvin, M.D. From a talk at Rodeph Shalom School, New York, NY and sent to the Alliance by Dr. Rosenfeld on February 27, 2004.

Smilansky, Sara. Sociodramatic play: Its relevance to behavior and achievement in school. In E. Klugman & S. Smilansky (Eds.), *Children's Play and Learning.* New York: Teacher's College Press, 1990.

Surgeon General. Summary of conference on children's mental health. Department of

Health and Human Services, 2001. Retrieved
1.29.03 from http://www.surgeongeneral.gov/
topics/cmh/childreport.htm#sum

Wilson, Frank. *The Hand.* New York: Pantheon,
1998.

ೲ

Joan Almon is the Coordinator of the U.S. branch of the Alliance for Childhood. She is a former Waldorf kindergarten teacher in North America and has worked internationally as a consultant to Waldorf educators and training programs.

The Genius of Play

Sally Jenkinson

Genius: attendant, tutelary spirit, et cetera (OED)

Using both recent research and published material, this article indicates something of the depth, breadth, and complexity of children's play. It draws a parallel between the creative play of early childhood and our relationship to art, literature, and drama as mature adults. It puts forward the argument that the imagination is both a vehicle for human creativity and a vital social force that leads us, through empathetic thinking and imitation, to the realm of the other. It argues that to deny children the right to play is to risk cultural, social, and personal deprivation.

Despite the existence of numerous excellent books and articles on the importance of children's play, the word "play" is still read, at least in the lexicon of educational policy makers, as the negative and polar opposite of "work." Play is regarded as a euphemism for idle, frivolous engagement, or for doing nothing; whereas, work suggests serious, purposeful activity. Work is worthy, play a mere diversion.

Start Right: Document on Nursery Education, written by Sir C. Ball and published in the United Kingdom in 1994, temporarily reconciled the work/play opposition by stating somewhat paradoxically: "Play is the serious work of childhood." Here at last, was a welcome endorsement of play, a recognition that children could be working and playing *at the same time*—a prin-

ciple that early-years educators have long known. It confirmed the notion that although much of children's play is light-hearted and full of charm, it is also earnest and worthy, with depth and dimension demanding our patient observation and respect. In George Eisen's moving and sometimes harrowing book, *Children and Play in the Holocaust*, Huizinga states, "Play is a thing by itself. The play concept, as such, is of a higher order than is seriousness. For seriousness seeks to exclude play, whereas play can very well include seriousness." (Eisen, 1990, p.7) Eisen argues that even children in such pitiful circumstances were unable to play in ways that were anything other than serious. That they still needed to play is perhaps the most poignant testimony to the importance of play—it effectively undermines the notion of play as a purely frivolous activity. Eisen himself regards the children's play—their games among the shadows—as one of the mysteries of that tragic epoch.

Play with a purpose?

It is now three years since *Start Right* was published, and suddenly a whole new set of targets, outcomes, and assessment criteria are in use. A dramatic shift in educational thinking has made work the leading educational impulse and once more the order of the day. Children busy playing at the serious work of your childhood—beware!

95

The pressing need to meet targets means that, for many institutions, play is either marginalized entirely or used exclusively as a learning tool. The cognitive "learn-as-you-play" model, which requires children to direct their play toward predetermined and specific outcomes, has clear educational advantages; children genuinely enjoy learning this way, and as a method of acquiring knowledge, it works. However, a diet of too much of this kind of "pre-cooked" play fare may deprive the child of the freshness, nourishment, and vibrancy of freely-chosen, open-ended play, and eventually dull the palate. As all good play-watchers know, the great fascination of really creative play is its unpredictability. The unexpected and sometimes astonishing twists and turns that make up the living journal of the day's play demonstrate the scope, profundity, and sheer energy of the childhood imagination which, in free play, "moves forward simultaneously in several planes of thought at once." (Lowenfeld, 1935, p. 177) To use play as a means to an end somehow misses the point of what it really has to offer, rather as if we were to read great literature solely as an aid to improving our spelling.

The Art of Play and Play as Art

What children actually do when they play is a complex and fascinating issue. Following the work of Lowenfeld, Drummond, Selleck and others, I would argue that part of what children represent in their play is an undifferentiated expression of what we later come to call art, literature, and drama. In a kind of perpetual metamorphosis, children move like quick-fire from the fantastic to the everyday and back again in the never-ending drama of "the play." They play as the spirit moves them—the same attendant spirit, I would suggest, that later inspires our creative expressions as adults.

An incident in my own kindergarten shows that in childhood the distinction between art and play is not easily made. A small boy had

been to see a dolphin over the weekend; an experience which had strongly moved him. On Monday morning, he came to the kindergarten like a poet suffering under his muse, with a burning desire to express and recreate his thoughts and feelings and to re-live his experience. With a sure touch, he took a long blue veil, spread it on the floor, lay upon it on his tummy, crossed his feet to make a tail, and gently waved his legs up and down. His participation was so absolute and his imitation so perfect that you could almost hear the water lapping about his feet. I felt as though I was witnessing the creation of a bodily poem or a beautiful piece of installation art. It was one small boy's personal homage to the dolphin that had so impressed him. Who can say where art begins and play ends? In the art of his play, his body and veil became his paint, palette, and canvas as, in his own "childish" way, he brought his deeply felt experience to exquisite expression.

Our Research

In a recent small-scale study for the Institute of Steiner Waldorf Education, a group of students were asked to study children at their free play. Our objective was to find out what they were actually playing and to classify some of the different types of play. One of the graduate students, Edward Marks, observed a group of twelve children at the Ringwood Waldorf kindergarten. Although such studies are prone to subjectivity, Edward strove to be rigorous and respectful in his methods. He never interfered, not even to ask questions, as he felt that any involvement on his part would subtly affect and alter the play. He was also aware that children have a surefire instinct for knowing when they are being watched and either play to the crowd or clam up completely, so he occupied himself with some small task, such as sewing, and made his notes discreetly. He aimed to be a friendly presence without disturbing the children. Creative playtime lasted for just over an hour and a half each morning, and over a period of eleven days,

Edward was able to observe almost seventeen hours of uninterrupted play. During this time, he recorded a total of fifty-four "themes," all of which were initiated by the children. The teacher also intervened as little as possible, only making helpful suggestions or giving direction when it seemed absolutely necessary.

The following list is a selection of some of the themes: horses and masters, cheese factory, paper factory, spaceship and dragon, really big house or castle, dark houses (with lantern), car journey (as mice), cooking, ironing, trains and engines, forest, cafe, big school, snakes (snake mommies, daddies, brothers and sisters, et cetera), insects, fishing, ferry boat, doll as baby, wizard of dark house, home-made "weeing" doll, having lots of visitors, shopping, and pussy cats.

The themes flowed into each other, involving different groups of children at different times, and allowing inspirations for play to rise and fall in a kind of co-operative dream of the imagination. New belief systems were invented and willingly adopted in a process which Coleridge understood as:

> "That willing suspension of disbelief for the moment, which constitutes poetic faith." (Biographia Literaria, Ch. 13)

Sometimes a theme would be played and then abandoned, to be revived later, occasionally not until the following day. Themes were played out in a variety of ways, which included socio-dramatic play, solitary play, exploratory play, play involving leaders and followers, and play following a "script" (for example, Peter Pan and Wendy made a brief appearance). There was also much reenactment of puppet stories, in which narrative, dialogue, and "set design'" all featured strongly. Puppets who fell over were repositioned, and ordered, by authorial command to "stay!"

The children usually named their games as a way of defining their subject and of signaling the start of a particular play. Naming the game also allowed everyone to enter the same imaginative sphere. Roles were allocated and characters defined and refined as the action progressed. This process of definition was very important to them; like the literary use of titles, chapter headings, and character delineation, it helped the children to establish a framework of meaning for their play narrative.

"We're mischievous mousies, yeah?" was the title and opening chapter of one game. Later on specific knowledge was added, such as what mousies eat and what threatens them (cheese and cats!). Further chapters included mousies getting into a car (with a basket for the steering wheel), mousies going shopping to buy food, and, inevitably, mousies being chased by cats.

Not only shared definitions but also agreement over what was permissible within a particular game needed to be established. Two boys had a conversation about whether or not a house, which they had already built, could or could not become a castle. After *lengthy* deliberations, they finally reached mutual agreement and decided that it could. These important social negotiations just do not happen at the solitary desk or worktable.

Some play was fleeting. For example, a piece of wood became a skillfully played saxophone in which the child's gestures faithfully recreated the original observation, even down to the smallest detail. Other play was sustained and complex. Children created a succession of worlds, which, though sometimes fantastic, nevertheless represented a coherent whole, each with its own symbolic structure and appropriate set of props. A particular spot was usually chosen to function as the doorway in a variety of different versions of the game of "house." This threshold became the agreed sign and symbol of boundary and ownership. The sanctity of the door as the central sustaining feature in games of house seems to be a universally recognized feature. Entry by any other route is simply not permitted; if children do start coming in through the walls, it usually signals the breakdown of the game. This was one of many self-imposed rules accepted by the group. A series of more tangible props also supported play activity. In the syntax of their play, these physical props functioned as instant, adaptable, and supremely interchangeable metaphors; buckeyes became matches, string became snakes, a hand-sized piece of wood became a cell phone.

The ability to endow an object with a different order of existence is a genuine talent of childhood. The child becomes the creator of the play object and invests something of herself in her creation; she has sought and found something there, a reflection of her own creative gift perhaps. Picasso mirrored this childhood activity with the playful art of the "found object," which opened new ways of seeing to the adult—something we could learn equally well from our children, if only we would look.

As well as giving life to objects, the children at Ringwood, sometimes alone and sometimes together, also created imaginary *worlds*. David Cohen (Cohen, 1987, p. 109) gives a lovely example of an imaginary world, or paracosm, called Gondal. This world, created by Charlotte and Emily Bronte, was full of dashingly romantic military officers! They believed they had learned how to devise interesting characters and plots through their youthful games with Gondal. It is stating the obvious to suggest that the inspirations which flow into the creations of such childhood worlds come from the same rich vein which we later tap when we write stories or poems. It is the imagination, after all, which creates good literature, not the ability to write letters.

(The use of the free imagination's possibility for moving beyond the confines of a difficult situation has also been a life-saving gift for those in captivity or in hiding, as Brian Keenan, John McCarthy, and many others have testified. Eisen's words speak for them all: "With the aid of make-believe one could symbolically demolish the physical confines of a little room or bunker." (Eisen 1996: p. 72)

In the Ringwood study, much of the play revolved around children "being" someone or something else. I would argue it is here that the genius of play begins to awaken social sensitivity and intuition at a very profound level through the playful activity of imaginative empathy. Some examples from the study: "You can be the big schoolgirl." (How do big schoolgirls feel, act?); "I'm a spaceship man." (How might a spaceship man behave? What fears might he have? How might he face up to challenges?); "This is the door of my kindergarten." (Now I can be as kind or as unpleasant as my own teacher.); "Are you a mouse?" "No, I'm a prince." (So you need to treat me very differently.); "What can I be?" (Whatever you wish!).

The question, "Who am I in this game?" and "How must I be as my new self?" is a major preoccupation for most young players. Through imaginative play, and in particular through socio-dramatic play, children are able to express and explore their own viewpoints and feelings, and as Jane Hislam perceptively observes, they are also able to explore *feelings that are not necessarily their own.* (Moyles, Hislam et al, 1994). In the magic of empathetic imitation, which is quite different from copying, children live imaginatively into the experience of the other. Then, guided by the inspirational spirit of play, the ability to "read" the thoughts and feelings of others begins to awaken, and the journey toward emotional literacy begins.

This capacity is absent in most children with autism. In his book, *The Development of Play*, David Cohen argues that although autistic children do play with objects—by moving them around and so on—they hardly ever engage in pretend or imaginative play. He suggests that this is because autistic children find it impossible to develop a theory of the other mind. Like adults with Asperger's syndrome, they might know what tears are, but not what they mean. Most autistic children are unable to perceive what another person might think or feel because, sadly, they are locked into their own worlds. (Cohen 1996:166).

Tina Bruce gives an example of a child who begins to explore, through unsentimental imitation, the very different thoughts, feelings, and experiences of someone else. "A new girl called Jo joined a nursery class. Jo had an artificial arm: two of the girls, Nadia and Jody, were fascinated when she took it off at story time because she did not want to wear it all the time. That afternoon, the children played together, and Nadia was Jo. Through her play, Nadia entered a world alternative to her own, in which she had no arms. She used all of her knowledge of what arms are for, and she came to know about Jo as she hadn't before." (Bruce, 1994, p. 117)

It is my belief, that through their own play, children can foster and develop the very qualities that will provide a powerful antidote to the "cultural alienation" that threatens our society today.

By trusting to the wise tutelage of the spirit of play, we educators can be partners in the creation of a social future. In the "quick, now, here, always" of their play, children are learning what it means to be human. They need our support and understanding in this most daunting of tasks. (Eliot, 1942)

Bibliography

Ball, Sir C. *Start Right Document*. RSA, 1994.

Bruce, Tina. *Time to Play in Early Childhood Education*. Hodder & Stoughton, 1994.

Cohen, D. *The Development of Play*. Routledge, 1993.

Drummond M. J. and Pollard, A. *Assessing Children's Learning*. David Fulton, 1993.

Eisen, G. *Children at Play in the Holocaust Games among the Shadows*. The University of Massachusetts Press, 1990.

Eliot, T. S. *The Complete Poems and Plays*. Faber and Faber, 1970.

Hislam, J, ed. by Moyles, J.R. *The Excellence of Play*. Open University Press, 1994.

Lowenfeld, M. *Play in Childhood*. Victor Gollancz, 1935.

Marks, E. *Observations of Children*. Unpublished material, 1997.

Selleck, D. et al. *Reflections on Early Education and Care*. BAECE, 1997.

Steiner, Rudolf. *The Education of the Child*. Anthroposophic Press, 1996.

Steiner, Rudolf. *The Gospel of St. Luke*. Rudolf Steiner Press, 1988.

☙

Sally Jenkinson is the author of The Genius of Play: Celebrating the Spirit of Childhood, *Hawthorne Press, 2001 and is currently researching a book for children and speaks, lectures and runs workshops on early years issues. Sally's background is in teaching and she has worked for the Steiner Waldorf Schools Fellowships. She was one of the founding members of the Alliance for Childhood, an international forum established to enable partnerships of organizations and individuals working to improve children's lives. She is married with three children and lives in England.*

Understanding Imitation through a Deeper Look at Human Development

Joop van Dam

The little child is a will being. The truth of this struck me when my little grandchild sat at the table and banged on it again and again with a spoon. He was placed on the floor, but continued to m ove his arm. So much movement—as if he were moving towards the future. Then he began going up the stairs, upwards, upwards until the moment came when he fell down the stairs, but that did not bother him. He began to climb again.

This is the will that is so associated with the body, but there is another will, too. It is like the other leg on which the child walks or the other wing with which it flies. This is the tremendous trust and confidence with which the child meets the world. This openness and trust is so great in the small child and is one of the reasons a very young child can seem so large. He embraces the world. A family went to visit friends who had a newborn baby. One of the visiting boys said to his little sister, "The baby is so small." "Oh, no," the girl said, "my brothers are small, but the baby is very big."

Imitation lives and moves in the child with these two legs or wings: that which opens to the world inwardly from the body and that which opens to the world in trust. Where do these two forces come from?

What do the scientists today say about the child? The old theories are disappearing. Before, it was said that children develop according to their instincts and drives. Then, the environment enters and the child learns to hold its instincts back. Out of this process conscience develops. Today, science acknowledges a third element that is most important. It has to do with the I, or individuality, of the child working through and finding its way in the world. This is the power of initiative that is there from the beginning.

American Professor of Psychology, Daniel N. Stern, MD, wrote an excellent book entitled *Diary of a Baby*. It describes how the baby is full of initiative from the beginning onwards. From the seventh month, the child begins to notice something in itself and also something in its mother. The child begins to seek its mother with full trust and confidence. She is the one who guides the child, and there is a time around the eighth or ninth month when the child wants only her mother. After this time, the child opens more widely again to others.

Through this trust, the child orients very strongly to human beings. He finds his way into the world as he gazes at the face of his mother. There is a very important law at work here— through other people the child develops his own individuality. Through the warmth of others, his own warmth develops. When I visited Monte Azul in the favela of Sao Paulo, the center developed by Ute Kramer, I was deeply impressed by the clinic where children are born. The mother and baby stay there for three days, and the fathers can also sleep there. It is a wonderful place, and for three days the infant can experience the world in its warmth and beauty. The child can open in full trust.

Between child and parent there is a very subtle but very important dialogue which takes place. The child begins the conversation when it comes down to earth to the parents. Rudolf Steiner, when lecturing in the Hague, said, "From the spiritual world the child has come to you." Now the mother can answer, and it is important that she does. She speaks, and how she speaks is of the greatest importance. It is not what she says that matters, but how she responds to her child. Modern science calls this the intuitive response of the parents. The child also has an intuition that arises from its will. The mother is able to perceive what her child needs. How does she do this? She does it through love. The child has a love for the whole world, and this is echoed by the love of the mother for the child. A deep love is created for this child who has selected her as a mother.

In this dialogue, there are two voices. The child begins, and the mother answers. Her being is a complement to the child's trust that helps the individuality of the child incarnate into the world in his or her body. Children are not fully in their bodies but hover above it, looking down on themselves. A man described two strong experiences he had which appeared to be memories of how he viewed himself from above as a child. In one, he saw a sand hill and he saw himself as a child climbing the hill, viewing it from above. On another occasion, he saw a grandfather with a baby on his lap and realized that he was the baby as seen from above.

The role of the mother, or guiding person, was observed by Dr. Spitz, who compared two children's homes. They were very similar in terms of hygiene, etc., but one was an orphanage for children without parents, while, in the other, the children were visited twice daily by their mothers who were in prison next door. What happened to the children? Those in the orphanage were much slower in their development. They learned to walk and talk much later than the children who saw their mothers regularly. A third of the orphans died before age six. They did not find their way into their bodies. A child needs a guiding person in order to incarnate into the body.

When I was a boy and was ill, my bed was moved next to my mother's. I welcomed this and expressed it by saying, "My mother sleeps me healthy again." Through this openness to the world and the subtle dialogue with the mother, the child finds its way to its own body, but Rudolf Steiner spoke of more than just the physical body. He also spoke of the etheric or life body, the astral body, and the I. What does it mean that the etheric is born around age seven? The etheric body has two aspects. One aspect has to do with the nature or natural side of the etheric that helps to build up the physical body.

There is also a cultural side, however, which relates to the development of consciousness, for it relates to memory and thinking. We experience this side when we are tired and find we can't remember things. It's easier to think in the morning when the etheric is refreshed.

The birth of the etheric in the child occurs in stages. During the first third of the first seven-year period, the etheric frees itself from the head. We see this in the children's drawings—all those circles! In the second third, the etheric of the middle system is born. Now rhythmic play begins, and one sees the middle realm develop in drawings. In the final third from roughly five to seven, the etheric frees itself from the limbs and metabolic system. Now the will develops much more strongly, and children stay with a task much longer. Also the question of death arises at this time. A five-year-old, for instance, spoke of "lebensmittel." This German word for food contains "leben" in it, which means life. "Lebensmittel," said the child, "That's what we eat so we don't die, right?" This is a typical remark of this age.

Also during this final third, the children enter their limbs more fully. We see them becoming school ready in areas of physical development, social life and thinking. Now the child wants to learn. It has occurred to me, while looking at the first grade of a school, how closely related to the kindergarten the first grade is. There is still much play, and also a fabric is being woven through storytelling. The stories being told are fairy tales the same as in the kindergarten. Fairy tales are stories with true pictures that arise out of the deeper essence of the human being. The inspiration for them came not through intellectual people, but through very simple people who heard the stories and repeated them. These are true fairy tales. There are also fairy tales that are thought out, in particular the Anderson fairy tales, but also stories by Tolkien and C. S. Lewis.

After hearing an Anderson fairy tale, a child said, "That story makes me so tired." Delicately, the adult asked, "Why don't the other fairy tales, like Hansel and Gretel, make you tired?" "Oh," said the child, "because they think like I think."

Sometimes, fairy tales are viewed from a soul or psychological point of view. Truths may be found this way, but fairy tales also have a physiological basis. For example, *Snow White and Rose Red* offers wonderful pictures of the forces of sympathy and antipathy. Snow White always maintains a distance. When she encounters the dwarf, she takes out her scissors and cuts off part of his beard. At night, it is she who closes the door of the house. She is the winter child. In contrast, Rose Red is the summer child who awakens early and goes out to pick flowers for her mother. She opens the door when there is a knocking. When she meets the dwarf, she

wants to fetch others to help. She is the outgoing one—full of the forces of sympathy.

The flowers she gathers are probably of all colors—they are as varied as all the processes in the digestive system: green like the gall, red like the blood, brown like the intestines. In *The Wolf and the Seven Little Kids*, when the wolf comes in, the seven goats hide. One hides in the washing bowl, one in the stove, one in the clock case, and so on. There are pictures hidden in the fairy tales, and one could also say: one hides in the kidneys, one in the liver, one in the heart, and so on. This joining of psychology and physiology means that the etheric forces, that are called upon when the fairy tale is told, are never torn away or "abstracted" from the body. After they have been in the consciousness (as consciousness-building forces), they find their way back to the physiological processes to which they belong and where they build the body.

Now let us return to the I, or ego, and the way it incarnates into the etheric body and through it to the physical body. It does so in three stages:

In the first 2 1/3 years, the senses awaken.

In the next 2 1/3 years, fantasy and play help build the body.

In the last 2 1/3 years, work and play related to adult work help build the body.

For all of this to happen, a special atmosphere is needed. It is an etheric atmosphere such as in a garden. This special garden atmosphere needs to be created in a kindergarten. How can we picture this? As we picture a plant, we see it going through its stages of growth from seed to plant to blossom to fruit. This takes time, and the nature of the etheric pertains to time. If something is to thrive, it takes time. Growth processes are also related to cosmic time and the working of the sun, moon and planets. Etheric time is also unhurried. Hurry comes from the astral body, which tells us, "Do this, do that, but before that, do this, and so on." Etheric processes need time for ripening—steady, constant time.

In my own childhood, life felt timeless and eternal. Now as a doctor, I find that when I have an appointment with a child and her family, I must be careful not to lose track of time. In the presence of a child I can easily let the appointment run much too long. This timelessness lives in fairy tales and can be heard in the closing line, "And if they have not died, they are still alive today," or "They lived happily ever after."

When one enters a Waldorf kindergarten, one can feel this etheric mood. Timelessness exists. It's like lying on a mountain meadow and "hearing the grass grow." One hears a certain hum in the kindergarten. During a transition time, the hum may stop, but then it begins again. The kindergarten teacher learns to work with this etheric atmosphere. If it feels too cold, she warms it. If it's too fast, she slows it, and if it's too slow, she quickens it.

In reviewing again the three phases of the first seven years, in the first phase, there are the sense impressions. Everything is taken in through the senses, and the physical should reflect the etheric. The season table is a picture of this with its changing array of shells, nuts, turnips with candles, and the many other things that find their way there through the year. It is life, a picture of Paradise. On the wall the Sistine Madonna or a fairy tale picture can hang, but it should have a timeless or eternal quality, such as the Sistine Madonna.

The clothing of the kindergarten teacher is also of great importance. The draping of Greek garments or the robes still worn in the Middle East by men are all a picture of the etheric body. This is also why angels are always portrayed with robes. In eurythmy, too, the garments worn reflect the etheric and have no division between the legs and not a strong division of the legs from the body as a whole. Clothes are associated with different forms of work and play an important role in life. This applies to the clothing of the kindergarten teacher, as well. Children remark on their softness, their color and other qualities.

In the second phase of early childhood, speech and language play an important part in building the physical body and also in the movement of the etheric body. The future intelligence of the child has to do with language that enters the etheric body and grows into intelligence. A rich language helps develop the body and the intelligence. Language arises in the child when the hands and arms are freed from locomotion. It is a creative process. From the Word, all is created.

When a word is full of pictures, a child experiences this and wants to speak it. This, too, builds the body. Hermien Yserman is a Dutch writer of children's books with a special relation to language. Children take great joy in her books and the wonderful way she uses words that come alive. Rudolf Steiner described this living aspect of a word in relationship to the German word for bath—*bad*. The sound of "b" surrounds us, the "ah" covers us with warm water, and the "d" encourages us to stay down in it.

One also feels the magic of the word in the Grimm's fairy tale of *The Little Hut in the Forest*, where a line is repeated several times: "My pretty hen, my pretty cock, my pretty brindled cow, what are you saying now." "Duks," they answered. "Duks" is not a word, but everyone understands it.

Another aspect of these middle rhythmic years is that dance is so important. It would be good if parents could do eurythmy with their children, for it builds organs. But what sort of eurythmy would this be? Not a eurythmy for the stage, but a special eurythmy that children could imitate. With a simple gesture, one can show a cat licking milk from a bowl. How the children enjoy the "m" for milk and for "meow."

Rudolf Steiner has compared children's growth with plant growth. Very small children are like mushrooms, for they are still asleep. Then come the ferns, and the kindergarten children are like the evergreens. Only in first grade, do we come to the flowering plant. For the kindergarten child, everything must still be in the green etheric realm. Their eurythmy must also be suited to them and not yet be dramatic. Drama begins to enter with the blossoming of the flowers, which is related to the astral realm. The little child is still living in the etheric realm and the growth forces connected to it. The children dip into the etheric and live there.

Today, there is so much of the dramatic already in the kindergarten child. They are blossoming prematurely. Let them sleep again, and this means engage them in "doing," for in the will we are asleep. Let them engage in all the wonderful activities like bread baking, cooking and the like. In olden times, people lived into their work and had time for it. In Laura Ingalls Wilder's books, she describes the wonderful rhythm of the housework that began with washing on Monday and ironing on Tuesday and ended with baking on Saturday and rest on Sunday.

Whenever children have the chance, they will eagerly watch a craftsman at work. They see the blacksmith, for instance, and drink in his gestures, and, later, they will play them out. These work gestures build the body. When a child has the opportunity to do many kinds of work in the first seven years, then she is able to build up her body in differentiated ways. Her body becomes

an instrument with all kinds of tones and colors. This is a body the individuality can enter and live in for a lifetime.

In conclusion, one can say that children today are born into a world practically without sheaths. The sheath of the family is not there as it once was. The sheath of the Church is largely gone. All such sheaths have disappeared, and this is appropriate, for this is a time of the individual. But for the child, it is a sheath-less world. One could say that the modern child is homeless.

What is being asked of us? First, to create new sheaths, to create a surrounding which is worthy of imitation. In addition, we can recognize that the child is homeless because it has another home, and that is in the spiritual world. The child comes to earth with a plan, an intention; she wants to do something here. Each has her own intention. The world is made young by these newborn children. It is continually made new. When we truly listen and hear, then we can help each other to realize our intentions.

If we know this, then a sound rings forth. Rudolf Steiner said, "The child has come out of the spiritual world to you. You need to solve its riddle from day to day and hour to hour. That is our work."

Joop van Dam was a physician in Holland and former General Secretary of the Anthroposophical Society in that country. He presented this lecture at an International Waldorf Kindergarten Conference in Eindhoven, Holland in October 1994 and was summarized by Joan Almon.

Readiness
for Kindergarten
and School

Kindergarten Readiness

Dr. Elisabeth Jacobi

The question of whether there is a time of "kindergarten readiness" has become an urgent question in Europe only in the last few years. Not long ago, in our experience, a child rarely came into the kindergarten before the end of his fourth year. There was no room. With the decline of the birthrate, however, an increasing number of kindergarten spaces has become available, and the younger children are entering to fill them. The kindergartens want to fill their places, and the mothers are glad to be able to bring their children into the kindergarten early. Thus, the age of the children who come into the kindergarten is now lowered to such a point that it is necessary to become clear about what constitutes kindergarten readiness in a child.

We want to disregard external necessities for bringing children into the kindergarten early—whether it be that the mother must go to work or that the atmosphere in the home is such that one would like to remove the child as soon as possible. The central question remains before us: How do I recognize whether a child is really ready for kindergarten?

In her speech, today's child often says "I" as early as two years old. In the etheric body, the child's head becomes independent around the age of two and a half, and she begins to think. But the "I experience" still does not fully happen today until the child is three years old. Only after this step has been fully accomplished does the child begin slowly to make verbal contact with other children. This is achieved at about four years of age. At this age, the remaining speech development is often already complete, but not always. Children who cannot yet pronounce g-k-ch sounds have difficulties in their will development; while children who have difficulty pronouncing s-sch-st are behind in their intellectual development in certain cases.

Much depends upon the parents' home when one considers the independence of the children. Whether a child can dress himself, whether he is clean, whether he can use the toilet independently is, to be sure, essential for the kindergartner, but these factors alone do not determine if the child has reached kindergarten readiness.

One must pay attention to the mental and physical stamina of the child. Can a child last four hours (the time of the normal kindergarten in Germany) without actually needing a nap? Is the child so susceptible that he would catch every sniffle in the kindergarten and become sick? Is the child already far enough along to handle the childhood diseases, or would it mean a premature exposure in certain cases? The child should already have developed a beginning sense of time. She must also have already overcome the first phase of defiance that still belongs to the "I" discovery. She must be able to tolerate other children, in particular, many other children.

A small child plays by himself, runs to the others, watches, perhaps takes something away and continues to play alone again even when many other children are in the room. The child is very imitative, but the imitation appears mostly from hours to days later rather than right away. Only when a child can imitate spontaneously and can play with other children, do I consider him ready for the kindergarten.

Painting and drawing depend again very strongly on how the child has been introduced to them at home. Recognizing kindergarten readiness is little agreed upon in this area unless one knows exactly the rules of how the development of a child is mirrored in the "language of drawing." But it is important for the kindergarten child to recognize danger. The child needs this ability, among other things, for the kindergarten walk. Also, a kindergarten child should generally already be able to go for a walk uninterruptedly without stopping at every little stone. A child should be able to refrain from fighting with another child as well.

When one examines the kindergarten child as a physician, one experiences a certain inner independence or even boldness in the child, and one has the impression that, yes, this child is in his place. A three-year-old or a younger child has almost a protective covering over himself which preserves him in his world. If one brings such a child into the kindergarten, then this covering rips open in about three weeks and a "plucked, featherless little bird" stands before us. This can happen even if the child visits the kindergarten on an hourly basis, and the torn covering cannot be repaired simply by removing the child from the kindergarten. This unveiling of the protective covering occurs naturally between three-and-a-half to four-years-old. Only then is the child really ready for the kindergarten. Whenever we cause this process to advance prematurely, we are doing something similar to the early learning of reading. Of course, a protected, veiled child brings a great deal of heavenly forces and warmth of soul to the kindergarten teachers. This leads to the latter expressing quite a special affection for the very young ones, but this is an area that naturally weaves itself between parent and child and, in particular, between mother and child. No one else ought to interfere directly with this. It is emphasized here once again that this is spoken from a physician's point of view, and that the social and social-pedagogical duties toward emergencies and families in stress have not been addressed.

So the question of kindergarten readiness is to be examined very earnestly each time. Neither commercial nor emotional points of view ought to play a role here, and, in itself, that the child is being urged into kindergarten should not be a decisive factor. The teacher shares especially in the responsibility for the child's health in the first seven years.

⚬

Dr. Elizabeth Jacobi was born in Dresden in 1944. She worked as a pediatrician in her own surgery from 1967 to 2000. From 1967 on, she has given a great deal of her energy and time working for the Therapeuticum Raphaelhaus Stuttgart.

The Birth of the Etheric: The Transformation of Growth Forces into Thinking Forces

Michaela Glöckler, MD

In anthroposophical medicine, we have a situation similar to one that exists in the Waldorf kindergarten. Rudolf Steiner and Ita Wegman gave many indications in about anthroposophical medicine that are very helpful, but they have to be re-examined year after year, so that a more and more detailed understanding can arise as to why a particular medicine is correct. It is the same in the Waldorf kindergarten. One can paint a room pink, hang a Sistine Madonna, have a basket of cloths, wood pieces, etc., learn a few stories and songs and feel this is a Waldorf kindergarten. However, one must keep going to understand the "why" of what one is doing, to try to differentiate and to develop the work further.

The etheric in the child has much to do with thinking. We can think constructively, and this is healthy; we can think with our healing and regenerative thoughts, for the life of thought in the older child and adult is the same as the growth forces that we see in the young child. These growth forces are transformed into thinking forces. If someone has knowledge, he can open the way for others to higher knowledge. Even if you're not an initiate, you will be able to find which results of spiritual research fit into life's reality. Rudolf Steiner said again and again, "Do not simply believe something—prove it!" Let us look at the results of spiritual research to under- stand the etheric forces in the child. It is possible to prove and work with the special quality of the etheric forces.

For the moment, this can be taken as a picture of the etheric forces and how they work:

Realm of thoughts   Conscious Life

Biological Life   Subconsciousness

The etheric forces are building up the body during pregnancy and after the birth up to the age of twenty-one. We are unconscious of their work in our physical body. As they are freed from their work on the physical body, however, they become active in the life of thought, and we can become conscious of them. For example, when the life processes or etheric forces are at work in the liver, we are unconscious of them, but the way we bring thoughts together rests in the upper, conscious realm. That realm we can look at quite well.

It takes time to build up the nerve and sense organs, and this process continues until age nine. The eye, for example, is not ripe until around

111

age eight. Perspective is not developed until that time. A nine-year-old can pour accurately into a cup from a pitcher because he can judge how far to hold them from his body. A preschooler can not do this for she has not yet developed perspective. If the eye is abused at a young age by watching television, which is two-dimensional, or through other means, then the organ is damaged. Some things can be repaired, but the basic organ cannot be changed.

Until the sixteenth year, the heart, circulation and lungs are developing. Children should not be trained for athletics until the rhythmic system is developed around age sixteen. Until age twenty-two, the bones are developing. There is a ripening of the hormonal and metabolic system. Thus, throughout the first eighteen or twenty-two years the body develops not as a whole but organ by organ, system by system. As we look at the development of the three systems of the physical body—the metabolic, the rhythmic, and the nerve-sense systems—we see that all three are affected by the three deeds which the child experiences in the first three years. The upright process and the walking, which come at the end of the first year, stimulate the development of the nerve-sense system. Speech development at the end of the second year helps the breathing and rhythmic system. The thinking process of the third year helps develop the metabolic-limb system. As children play at this time, their hands and feet become more skillful, and they are learning to build and rebuild.

From one point of view, it is the nervous system that is developing in the first seven years, and in the case of the rhythmic system, the development takes place primarily between seven and fourteen. In the case of the metabolic system its development culminates between fourteen and twenty-one. Therefore in the grades, from ages seven to fourteen, the teacher reaches the students by using speech in such a manner that their feelings are touched. Speech stimulates sympathy and antipathy, and this

stimulates the ripening of the rhythmic organs, the heart and the lungs.

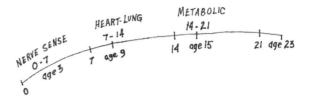

The above diagram may seem confusing, because we usually speak of the young child in the first seven years as working with the will-metabolic system. This is true, but while we say that the first seven years are the will period, we also say that the young child is a sense organ. The nervous system develops through physical movement. Ordinary medicine understands this and prescribes gymnastics for stimulating the nervous system of brain-damaged children. Until age nine, the child should move and be active as much as possible in order to develop his thinking. The kindergarten teacher relies upon movement in order to teach the young child, and it is movement that helps the child to develop the nerve-sense system. Movement is the best education for stimulating the brain.

At birth, the physical body is born, but it is only at age three that the body is used as an instrument for the I. At age seven, the etheric body is born, but it takes two or three years for the etheric to become an instrument. At age fourteen, the astral body is born, but only around age sixteen or seventeen does one have command over one's feelings. Likewise at age twenty-one, the ego is born, but only around age twenty-three does one begin to take life seriously. It always takes a few years after the birth of a body for it to begin functioning with a sense of mastery.

Let us look at the development of the adolescent. From age fourteen on, the young person is developing thoughts that are free of sense pictures. From sixteen on, the teen-ager can become very idealistic. He no longer needs teachers to tell him facts and to ask him to believe. He becomes his own master. If the organs of will have ripened, then this ripening of thought processes takes place around age sixteen. There develops an ability to judge and weigh, and this ability arises out of the grown-up metabolic forces.

If you look at the ripened thoughts of adults, you will see that the adult needs the possibility of self guidance in thought life; the adult "walks" in his thinking. He also needs "feeling" in his thought life. He must consider, for example, whether a thought is a pleasant or unpleasant one, and he also needs pictures in his thought life. This now becomes pure thinking activity, and the adult can find the laws of how things run. All that came before now fits together step by step, and, in these ways the different systems—the metabolic, the rhythmic, and the nerve-sense—help each other to develop.

When we look at the long-term development of the human being from birth to age sixty, we see the following patterns. The body is undergoing intensive growth in the first twenty years. Then come twenty years of relative stability in the body, and from age forty to sixty, the bodily forces begin to decline, and the body grows weaker and weaker.

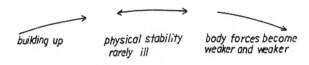

building up   physical stability   body forces become
                rarely ill   weaker and weaker

0–20 The life of thoughts increase year after year as the physical forces are freed for thinking.

20–40 A time of equilibrium during which one does not realize so strongly one's changes and growth.

40+ In getting older, the spiritual forces may increase more and more while the physical forces may decline.

Dr. Raymond Moody's books on near-death experiences show that when one is near death, one experiences tremendous clarity of thought.

Death is the moment of purest clarity and awareness.

What about the etheric forces in the life of the kindergarten child? Life wisdom is contained in the etheric. One should not imagine the etheric as a pleasant cloud, all rosy and hazy. The etheric is the body of wisdom and truth. The etheric forces are engaged in building up the body. Lies destroy the wisdom and life of the human being and hurt the etheric. All that is untrue harms the young child. Therefore, we must build an environment based on truth and integrity for the child.

The kindergarten morning should be viewed as an organism, like a body, in which all the organs fit together. One part of the morning should smoothly fit together with another. This fits with the way the etheric forces work.

Our etheric forces arise from the spiritual world. They come out of the relations of spiritual beings in that higher world. Imagine two angels with a certain relationship to each other. This is a tremendously active process, and out of this come our etheric forces. Therefore, with our thoughts, we can touch all beings of the world. We know when someone is thinking negatively of us, for we are etherically touched. Imagine if higher beings are thinking—what a powerful force is released. This is all reflected in our thoughts. We reflect this higher wisdom; we do not carry it within us. We reflect it, and this is our first relationship with higher knowledge.

The child experiences us as examples, and he experiences that we have etheric relationships. If the child feels in our gestures that we care for the physical world, she responds to that. We reveal our relationships through our daily activities. We create such a morning for the children. We take all things in earnest—with joy or sorrow. If we wash the dishes and wish we were outside, then the child feels that our actions are untrue and that there is something schizophrenic happening. If we like our work and feel it is useful, then the child feels this and responds to it.

The etheric body must keep regenerating. For example, every day with our bowel movements we lose six to seven ounces of cell substance that must be replaced. There are many, many cells that die each day, and the etheric body must keep regenerating new cells for us. It cannot refuse to do so. Likewise, we cannot say, "Today, I won't clean up." We repeat again and again that which is necessary in order to help the etheric body to do its work.

Art is a means of regenerating. An artist works again and again on his art and always sees ways to do it better. It is an expression of inner forces. We need to do our own artistic activity every day. We cannot simply "eat" the creativity of others. Through creative fantasy, every human deed can be transformed and made more beautiful. This is a process of self-training. To work with young children we must become small, humorous artists.

Our movements should have a creative, purposeful quality—they should not just be mechanical. As kindergarten teachers we should study eurythmy as much as possible, for we need more than just the outer form of gesture. Eurythmy movements are permeated with life forces.

Children whose speech process is disturbed need exercise. This is also the case with children who speak too much or at the wrong times. This is the same disturbance, but from two different sides. Such children should be brought into tranquility. We should teach parents to place their child on their laps and recite clear, well-spoken verses to him or her.

Our own character and will impulses give qualities of a specialized nature to our movements. Through our will, we bring an impulse into our movements; through our soul we bring a quality; and through our spirit, we bring meaning. In this true relationship of all things in the world, the child builds up a healthy, well-formed organism—an organization of wisdom. Then there is independence for new steps to be taken in adulthood and an interest in all things that exist in the world. Both are necessary.

Q: Can you speak of the relationship of fantasy to imagination?

A: The etheric forces work on the physical body, which gradually are freed to become thinking forces. On the way, they pass the realm of feelings, of inner soul forces, and take on the quality of fantasy. (Rudolf Steiner: "Fantasy is growth force projected into the soul realm.") As it comes more towards the brain and the thinking forces, the fantasy becomes more frozen, for then it is a dying process. We look at a person, and it is an etheric process that makes an impression through the eye on our etheric body. This is how we remember our impressions. It is a dying process. The pictures become fixed and must die so there is room for something new. These dying thoughts help us to arrange ourselves in the world, but are not a help to the inner life. For our spiritual possibilities, we need to keep the power of fantasy alive. Otherwise, our whole being will be affected by the dying process. This is why fairy tales are important. In fairy tales, there are fantasy pictures that are taken as seeds into our unconscious life which arise later as thoughts of the inner life.

Regarding the development of the child's organism, one can look into physiology books and learn about the development of each organ, for each has its own growth curve. We then need to put this together with the facts of spiritual development.

The most important fact about the education of the child in the first nine or ten years is that movement stimulates the nerve-sense system. Every skilled movement stimulates the brain, because the brain is "exercised." It has to notice all the movements and activities. It is not the "intelligent speech" of the adults which stimulates the child's brain, but the child's own activity. We should work with parents to help them understand this. The "intelligence of the body" is the basis for the "intelligence of the brain."

Q: Please speak about speech problems in young children.

A: It is important that we love speech and that our words are spoken like living beings. They must have sense, but they are not just information carriers. Children who stutter can often overcome this problem later in life if they are motivated to do so. When a three-year-old stutters, the problem in most cases (about 95%) will pass away by itself. Take time and listen, but don't ask the child to repeat. Before school age, all speech training should be in play form such as through verses, singing, and speaking—spoken clearly and not too fast. Most of these children do not need any additional professional help at the preschool age.

Q: What about problems of masturbation in young children?

A: This is a problem of the environment. If the child is not interested in its surrounding, then the child will take interest in the physical body. One should do something in hopes that it will interest the child. A way of healing is to engage the child in becoming active in the surroundings.

Q: In regard to warmth forces and warm clothing, what should be done about children who resist wearing warm clothing?

A: We see more and more children with weak constitutions who can be helped with the proper clothing. In particular, they need many layers in the trunk area (chest, stomach and back) for that is the area of the inner organs, which need the most warmth. When the trunk is warm enough, then the hands and feet will also receive enough circulation. The limbs are always cooler than the middle realm (28 C compared to 37 C.) Some children do resist warm clothing. Perhaps the clothing is made of synthetic fibers. It is very uncomfortable to be warm in synthetic clothing. Also, in about 70% of the cases, the child may be resisting as a form of provocation!

Q: What about children from single parent homes?

A: One hears about special concerns for children, especially boys, who live with a mother in a single parent home, but usually such children find their own male figures in life, possibly an uncle, grandfather or neighbor. One can place them with a male teacher, but they may not accept the male as a special role model.

Mixed age groups can be helpful for such children, as well as all children, for they can function like a family. The younger children look up to the older ones to see where they are going in their own development, while the older ones look back to see where they have come from. The teacher needs to differentiate between the different ages and create an artistic flow. The assistant can be brought into this process as well. The group integrated by age is best for the child.

Parents should be helped to keep at least five minutes of awareness each day for each of their children. Likewise, in the kindergarten, a teacher should have a personal moment with each child once or twice a week.

Many children today need healing work with a doctor or a curative eurythmist. In anthroposophy we have the knowledge of how to help children, but we do not have enough personnel. As teachers we must broaden our knowledge, but we mustn't try to substitute for another profession. We need to work together cooperatively. If one does not have an anthroposophic doctor in one's community, then seek a relationship with a doctor from another community. This allows one to call him or her and describe a symptom that's been discovered in a child and seek advice. In this way we are building up a new social fabric, which is so necessary here.

Q: How do we help children meet the many problems that they face in our modern times?

A: As we build up an awareness of our times, some people paint very dark pictures, indeed. Of course, there are many problems. We can see the problems of modern foods coupled with ecological problems and how they are resulting in allergies in children. We can see that children sit far too much and are not engaged in their will enough. We know that children should see the world at many different distances and that when they sit in front of the television they are taking it in from only one distance. We see many other problems which television brings to children. For example, children see only the outer aspect of the person on television, not the ego of the person. Most of the senses, especially the higher ones, are not engaged. Thus, television has a disintegrative effect on children rather than helping to bring about integration.

In the area of diet, we see the problems of children who consume sugar in significant amounts. Sugar is easily digested in the digestive tract. It takes no energy to do so. One does not even need a stomach to digest sugar, whereas, if one has to make sugar out of more complex foods such as bread, then it takes huge amounts of energy to digest it. It takes work to create the sugar. Eating sugar is rather like the drug process. There is one little injection and then a whole experience, a whole story begins. It is done so easily and with so little effort.

We also see many sleep disorders in people today. People have trouble digesting their life experiences and this leads to sleep problems.

Then they use sleeping drugs that make them half-asleep in the daytime and half asleep at night.

Anthroposophy arose in this century to help us understand every problem of our times. Without these problems, we would not be able to find our way to freedom. We would not need Anthroposophy. These problems are related to the development of freedom and, in this sense, area gift. We must remember that pursuing freedom without some error is not possible.

We must come to appreciate, even to love, the dark areas of life, for the new possibilities that arise from them. In this way, we can develop these Christian and human aspects. We should not say, "Waldorf education forbids television." Rather, it is an effort to understand at what age it is a healthy impulse and at what age it is not. After age sixteen, watching television is not a problem for the body and soul.

Regarding vaccinations, know what possibilities of development do not take place with vaccination. When parents learn about this, they are often sad and want to find a way to overcome the limitations of vaccination. The body can be stimulated from the spiritual side, from the life of thought and the world of fairy tales. The etheric works on the body from the inside and through the stimulating factors of the outside.

When we look at the most dangerous aspects of our time, we see important hindrances arising in our will, in our emotional life and in our thoughts. In the realm of will, modern human beings have become very inactive, and when we are inactive, we begin to mock and even hate those who are active. The healing antidote to this is our own activity. In the realm of feeling, we hide jealousy and even hate under a banner of criticism, and we have become a society of critics. All of this arises from a fear impulse. We are afraid of the ability of others, and we fear our own selves. We can overcome the obstacle of fear by developing interest in others. From this interest, love arises. Sympathy is not love, though many think it is, for sympathy changes too easily. In the thinking realm, no culture has as many "lies" in it as ours has. It begins with the automatic question of "How are you?" when one has no interest in the answer, and the lie goes on from there into advertising and many other realms of life that are based upon the lie. The healing for the lie is to love the truth.

The conditions of our modern life

We must aim for the path of activity, of interest and love, and of truth. This is a path that leads us toward freedom, and this is the path of Christianity. In a kindergarten atmosphere that is permeated with the teacher's striving in these areas, the children can develop their individuality and thereby find the strength to overcome the difficulties of the times.

Will	Emotional Feelings	Thoughts
↑	↑	↑
Inactivity	Fear	Lie
↑	↑	↑
Activity	Love Interest	Truth

☙

Dr. Michaela Glöckler is currently the head of the Medical Section at the Goetheanum in Dornach, Switzerland. She has been active as a pediatrician and school doctor in Germany and is the author of A Guide to Child Health, *Floris Books.*

First Grade Readiness

Joan Almon

What does it mean when we say that a child shows the signs of first grade readiness, or as the Germans so wisely say, that a child is *schulreif* (ripe for school)? There are many changes in the child's physical, emotional, social and mental life that one looks for, which can be listed and observed in a fairly objective manner. But there is also a *qualitative* difference that is more difficult to describe, yet very important to sense. The good gardener knows from one day to the next when a piece of fruit is ripe for picking, and when this process is translated into childhood, it relates to Rudolf Steiner's statement that a whole new aspect of the individuality is born around the age of six or seven. This new birth is not as physical and clear-cut as the physical birth of the child, but it is an important time in the growth of the child. It is the underlying reality for the many changes that are visible around ages six to seven.

To understand how such a birth can be part of the ongoing life of the child requires an image of human development that goes beyond linear growth and includes the image of transformative growth. Linear growth takes place along a continuum, and one can think of the line of growth as going on a steady incline upwards. Thus, one sees the child growing before one's eyes and can plot the line of growth by measuring height and weight, for instance. Transformative growth,

however, takes linear growth into account but goes a step further. It indicates that at certain critical points in an individual's development, a transformation takes place analogous to the caterpillar spinning a cocoon and emerging as quite a new creature, a butterfly. There are points in life when we enter a cocoon-like womb, go through many changes and emerge with a new form. Now we can fly in areas where before we could only crawl. One of these transformative stages of growth takes place at around age seven. At this time, Steiner describes the birth of a new body, which he calls the life body or etheric body. He goes on to describe two more periods of birth in the growing individual. The next is around age fourteen when the body of feelings, called the astral body, is born. And then, at around age twenty-one, the Ego or individuality comes to birth. All of these are present in the human being from the embryological stage, but they are in protective sheaths in which they grow like the embryo in the womb until their time of birth is at hand.

The etheric body, which is born at around age seven, parallels our physical body in many ways, but it is much subtler in nature. It is not visible to most human beings, but nevertheless plays a vital role in keeping the physical body alive and healthy. When the etheric body is weakened, as it so often is in modern human beings, we experience it as a weakening of the protective sheath which normally prevents illness from taking hold in the physical body. In this function, it bears a close relationship to the immune system.

With this background in mind, it is easier to understand school readiness, for after the birth of the etheric, the child is quite different than she was before. She is ready to fly in new areas, or, better said, she stands upon the earth in a new way. She seems so ready to *receive* knowledge from a figure of loving authority, whereas before she took in life through imitation. She offered her love to parents and to teachers and wanted to imitate them in all that they did and all that they felt, but she did not look to them for knowledge in the way she now does. One sees that she has developed new *capacities* needed for learning and absorbing knowledge. In her feeling life and in her rhythmic system she shows new capacities, as well, and seeks out friends with whom she can have deeper, more long-lasting relationships. Imagination is born in her and wants to be fed with stories and pictures. Physically, too, many changes have occurred, and in the child's movements, one sees a penetration into hands and feet that was not there before. The unique individuality of the child is still clearly recognized, but the body in which it is housed has gone through considerable change. In my experience, one usually sees these changes taking place over a period of about one year. It is a gradual process, but there comes a time when one looks at the child and senses that something really new has happened.

In a lecture on first grade readiness given at a conference in Lexington, Massachusetts, Dr. Gerald Karnow of Spring Valley, NY spoke of the etheric body in relation to the phantom limb experience of the amputee. Often after a limb has been amputated, the individual still "feels" the limb as if it were there. This is called the phantom limb. Unlike the physical limb, however, the phantom limb has some unusual characteristics. Amputees describe how they can contract the

limb and make it very small or enlarge it. They can project it through walls, for it knows no physical barriers such as physical limbs know. Dr. Karnow reported that patients with leprosy describe the differences between limbs which had to be amputated because of infection and those which had atrophied and needed to be removed. They described the latter as having *died* and reported no phantom limb phenomena with those, suggesting that the life body of the limb had died along with the limb. An example was also given of a child whose phantom limb was "born" around age six. She had lost an arm as a young child and had no experience of a phantom limb until around age six when she "grew" one. She spoke of how she could now use it for counting on her fingers.

The implication of these examples is that the etheric body is a real body, only not a densely physical one. It has its own nature and experience, its own birth and death. Rudolf Steiner speaks of the birth of the etheric as a necessary step before the child is introduced to academic subjects, for it is only with the birth of the etheric that memory is freed and the capacity for imagination is born. Both of these are needed for creative, healthy learning, and we will describe this process in more detail. Premature exposure to academic studies places a great strain on young children, as is finally being recognized by American educators and parents. Five-year-olds tend to be quite awake mentally, so it can seem that they are ready for some academic instruction. However, long-term studies indicate that they will not do as well in academic work or in other areas of life as those children who have been allowed to engage in healthy creative play until first grade readiness is established.

One such study was done in Germany in the mid-1970s. At that time, the thrust for early academics in the state kindergartens was in full swing, and most kindergartens in Germany had switched to being academic-oriented. Fortunately some German professors decided to study the results of such programs while there were still play-oriented kindergartens left for comparison. A study was done of fifty kindergarten classes that were play-oriented and fifty that were academic-oriented. Thus, about one thousand children from each type of kindergarten were studied. Their progress was followed through fourth grade, and it was found that the children from the play-oriented kindergartens excelled over the children from the academic-oriented kindergartens in every area studied—in physical development, emotional and social development, as well as in mental development. The results of the study were so impressive that the German kindergartens switched back to being play-oriented. (*Der Spiegel*, 1977, #20, pp. 89-90.) Unfortunately, a comparable large scale study was never done in North America, and early academics continued for nearly twenty years until the obvious stress in the children and their failure to succeed over the long-run convinced educators that academic kindergartens were a mistake. Although most American educators are now convinced that play-oriented kindergartens are very important for children, the prevalence of academics in the public kindergartens continues, for it takes many years for new ideas to filter down into the classrooms and drive the old practices out.

James Uphoff and June Gilmore have reported on other studies that indicate the difficulty of children starting school too soon. They used age cut-off as their criteria and found that "summer birthday" children who started kindergarten under the age of five years three months or first grade under six years three months tended to have greater difficulties than the older children in the classes. The problems manifested in a number of areas. The younger children tended not to do as well in their grades or on their scores on standardized tests. They tended to repeat a grade more often than did the older children, and they showed signs of learning disabilities more frequently. The academic problems of the younger children often lasted right into adoles-

cence and even into adulthood. The most disturbing part of the article by Uphoff and Gilmore was a report on a pilot study that they did on adolescents and young adults who committed suicide in their county in one year. Looking back at their schooling patterns, they found that a disproportionate number of them had started first grade under six years three months. This was especially true of the girls who had committed suicide, leading one to wonder if the boys found more ways to act out their frustrations in school, whereas the girls were more apt to bottle it up inside. At any rate, the findings of Uphoff and Gilmore lend a serious weight to considerations of first grade readiness. This is not simply an academic question of when a child should begin first grade, but is a decision that strongly influences the life of the youngster during the school years and beyond.

A few examples may help flesh out these findings. During a discussion about first grade readiness, a kindergarten teacher spoke of her own son who had started first grade long before she and her husband knew of Waldorf education. For the first few months of school, he came home each day in tears, obviously exhausted by the experience. His parents were unsure of what to do, but gradually he seemed better able to cope, and from second grade on, he seemed to be doing all right. Once the son was in twelfth grade, his father remarked one day that he must be happy to be graduating and going to college. Quite spontaneously, the young man answered, "No, I wish I had another year of school." The parents were stunned to realize that, although the boy had seemed to adjust to school, he had never felt completely at home with his placement there and should probably have waited another year before entering first grade. When we asked how the boy was doing now in adulthood, his mother went on to say that at age nineteen he was in a serious accident and nearly lost his life. Tragic as it was, it had the positive effect of helping him to find his rightful place within himself, and he seemed much better synchronized within himself after the accident. David Elkind, in his books, points out that children who have been hurried in life often need to take a year off after high school to catch up with themselves. This is one way to help overcome the stresses of too much academics too soon in life. But, Elkind points out that some of those who have been "mis-educated" have experienced stress at such a deep level that additional help is needed. In Waldorf education, we see that one source of this help is through artistic outlets or curative eurythmy. The arts, when presented in a healthy, living manner, help to promote healing.

Another example illustrates the relationship between readiness and learning disabilities. It involves a little girl who had been a borderline case as far as readiness was concerned. Both her teacher and her parents were undecided if she was ready for first grade, but at last decided she was and sent her on to a Waldorf first grade. She soon showed signs of difficulty and could not keep up with her class. Whereas some children might have acted out and misbehaved in these circumstances, her response was to become excessively dreamy. By winter, she seemed so unfocused in her work that her teacher grew concerned that the child had a learning problem and recommended testing. The testing service diagnosed serious learning disabilities and recommended she attend a special school for learning disabled children. They did not feel a Waldorf school could meet her needs, even with tutoring. They also recommended a quieter, more rhythmic lifestyle for the child, and in order to provide this, the parents decided to move to a smaller town with a Waldorf school for their younger child and a special school for their older child. Meanwhile, as she was gaining so little from her first grade experience, she returned to the kindergarten for the spring term and happily played for a few months. In the summer, the family moved and after much debate as to what would be best, decided to try the child again in the Waldorf school before enrolling her in the special school. They placed her in first grade again

to see whether she could possibly manage. It was soon apparent that the child showed no signs of learning disability at all. She mastered the first grade curriculum with ease and continued as an attentive, active student who is now in the fifth grade. Her only "learning problem" was that she had been placed in a first grade too soon.

It is painful to think of all the children who have unnecessarily suffered academically or personally simply because adults made poor judgments regarding their schooling. This has been a problem for some of the children in our Waldorf schools who entered first grade too soon, and it is not too late to help these children. By repeating a grade, they can sometimes be placed in the right situation. When parents and adults carry the responsibility for the "mistaken placement," the burden is removed from the child who need not feel any sense of failure. While not every child with school difficulties needs this solution, it is worth considering in some instances.

Serious as misplacement can be in a Waldorf school, these children were at least not being asked to do academic work before first grade. When one considers all of the American public school children who have been asked to do first grade work while in kindergarten during the past twenty years, one feels deep concern for the problems these children may suffer in their lifetimes. Already one hears of much greater stress among preschoolers, of burn-out among elementary children, and of high school students who seem unable to think creatively. In addition, many problems of adolescence have increased radically during the past twenty years, such as drug and alcohol use, teen pregnancies, teenage suicide, eating disorders and other forms of mental diseases. It is easy to imagine that unreasonable demands in schooling at young ages lead to stress which continues to escalate throughout the school years, leading to serious problems in adolescence, that most vulnerable of times. Of course, other problems such as family disturbances and excessive exposure to media also contribute to childhood stress, but the one area which the schools can more or less control is their own curriculum, and that is where immediate change is needed.

While contemporary research points out the difficulties of introducing academic work too soon to children, other research, such as that done by Sara Smilansky, shows the positive gains in academic and social areas among children who are strong in creative, fantasy play in their kindergarten years. One hopes that a more enlightened attitude will prevail in America and other countries in the coming years and that parents and educators will insist on academics being removed from the kindergarten and put back in the first grade where they belong. This "push down" of curriculum took place after the Sputnik scare of the 1950's. Now that the Cold War is over, surely this vestige of it in American education can be removed. If a healthy division between kindergarten and elementary education can be reinstated, focus can then turn to the fundamental question of when is a child ready to enter elementary school. What are the signs of first grade readiness?

In the physical realm, as in other realms, one sees many signs of change. Generally, there is a kindergarten "look" in contrast to a first grade "look," and this look has much to do with body proportion, for the limbs now stretch in relation to the body and head. There is also a loss of baby fat, and greater definition occurs in the face, which usually accompanies the loss of baby teeth. As the six-year-old molars come in, as well as the permanent teeth in the front, the jaw begins to grow to make more room for the molars and the second teeth. At this time, the chin becomes more pronounced, and the face takes on a more "down to earth" look. All in all, one sees less of a dreamy kindergartner and more of a focused first grader. One cannot see the changes as clearly in children who have thinned down at an earlier age and whose faces look "old" even in kindergarten, as on can in children with

the classic round look of the kindergarten child. However, even in the thin, wiry child close observation will show some changes.

Sometimes one sees a child in first grade who still has the classic look of a kindergarten child. It is well worth considering if this child has been misplaced. In one school, I was asked to observe a first grade where the teacher thought that one or two children belonged in the kindergarten. Simple observation showed that there were two girls who still had the "look" of kindergarten children. After further study of them, it was decided that one girl was well placed, but that the other should return to the kindergarten. Even though she was able to keep up with her class, it was noted that she could do so only by pushing herself to a great extent, and it was felt that this would take its toll over time. Another aspect of her development could be seen in her drawings. Her people and houses were well formed and looked like first grade ready pictures, but the people were not yet standing on the earth. Rather, they hovered in the air, about an inch above the grass line. We shall speak of children's drawings further on. The child's parents were concerned that she might feel she had "failed" first grade, but when she was told she would return to the kindergarten, her immediate response was, "Oh good, can I go back for Advent?" She reentered the kindergarten happily and is now in sixth grade and doing very well.

In the emotional realm, one feels how the emotional or soul life of the child is developing. While young children often show strong emotions, their emotional outbursts are like squalls that arise quickly and pass quickly. One moment the child expresses tremendous anger, saying how much he hates the adult and wishes he was dead, and in the next moment all is forgotten and the child is happily at play. Regrettably, adults tend to take such outbursts rather seriously and attribute more meaning to them than they should. Young children have strong feelings, but on a rather surface level. As the child approaches first grade readiness, however, the feelings begin to deepen. Now children complain of "hurt feelings" and will sit sadly for a while nursing these bruised feelings. In general, it is as if a hidden chamber has been found, where the feeling life dwells. There feelings of all kinds live, and these feelings have longer life and more depth than those of the younger child. The children sense that this chamber is a hidden room and more private, and a hidden side of the child begins to manifest. They love secrets and frequently will whisper them to one another. They like to play tricks and be sly and cunning in their behavior. They also become more aware of dreams and connect more fully with stories and artistic activities.

This new emotional life shows itself in social situations as well. The very young child engages in parallel play where he plays next to another child, but is not very involved with the child. The three- and four-year-olds play with "playmates" and engage actively with them during play situations, but tend not to think much about them otherwise. A common exception to this is with children whose families are close friends or where the children carpool together. Sometimes, too, what looks like an early friendship is simply a dependent relationship formed because a child is shy and needs a cohort for strength. Generally, however, three- and four-year-old children who find one another in the kindergarten have a lighter, short-term relationship with each other that we can call the playmate stage. The child getting ready for first grade, however, begins to form friendships that go deeper than these earlier stages. A friend is someone you think about even when you're not with the person. You care about them and feel loyalty towards them. Children at this stage begin exploring friendship. They love to invite children over or be invited to the homes of others. Parents joke that they need to keep social calendars for their children at this stage. Usually, one needs to establish some healthy limits on socializing of outside school, for, if left to the child, she may want to get to-

gether with other children four or five afternoons a week plus weekends. Such a busy social life would wear her out, to say nothing of her poor parents who have to chauffeur her about.

In the *mental realm*, several very important changes take place. One is the birth of memory, that Rudolf Steiner often refers to in relationship to the birth of the etheric body. This can be a confusing point, for parents are often amazed at how strong the memory of a young child can be. It is different, however, from the "freed" memory of the school child. The difference can be described in this way. If you ask a four- year-old if he remembers Grandma's birthday last year, he will probably look quite blank. But if you are baking a cake for the birthday party, and it is the same cake you baked last year, the sight of it may trigger the child's memory, and he will tell you about the party in remarkable detail. Or you may ask this child what he did in school and receive as the answer, "Nothing, we just played." While you're cooking dinner, one of the foods may trigger his memory of kindergarten snack, and suddenly you'll hear all about the kindergarten morning. Or you may ask what songs were sung at circle time and receive a perplexed look from the young child. Later, while he's at play, a melody goes through his mind, and suddenly he is singing and reciting the whole of the morning circle. Memory exists in the young child, but the child does not have free access to it. It takes something from the outside such as a sight or smell or a rhythmic verse from within to trigger memory that then comes pouring out in rich detail.

When memory is freed at around age six or seven, however, the child can freely enter in and find the memory he is looking for. The process reminds me of going into a large library and finding just the book one is searching for. A nine-year-old demonstrated this search to me when I saw him in a supermarket one day and asked if he remembered Acorn Hill, the Waldorf kindergarten he had attended. He clapped his hand on his forehead, closed his eyes and had a look of extreme concentration. After a minute or two, his brow cleared and he described a birthday celebration and an eurythmy class at Acorn Hill. He apologized for taking so long to remember his kindergarten but explained in great seriousness that he had gone to two public schools since then. I had a strong impression of his going into the library of his mind and going past the first shelves which contained his most recent school memories, past the next shelves which held his last school, and finally arriving at the Acorn Hill shelves.

Another aspect of mental change is in the realm of *imagination*, which is different from the *fantasy* of the kindergarten child. A characteristic of fantasy play is that the child needs props to carry out the play. It can be the very simplest of props such as children use in the Waldorf kindergarten, such as using corn cobs or small logs for baby bottles or stones and nuts for food, but it is hard for the four-year-old to feed her "baby" without some sort of prop at hand. When imagination is born, however, one often sees children play without objects. They can now "see" their play situation in their mind's eye and do not need the physical toys. I recall as a school child playing ongoing "soap operas" where we used no props at all, but the characters were fully alive in our minds. Bronja Zahlingen, a much-loved Waldorf kindergarten teacher from Vienna, describes her transition to imaginative play from fantasy play in this way: As a child she loved to play with small objects—people, houses, animals, etc.—on a deep window seat in her bedroom. She would create a scene and play with it by the hour. One day, when she had turned six, she set up a scene, as usual, but then closed her eyes and played the whole scene out in her mind. This is the birth of imagination. Sometimes a child will voice this change by saying something like, "I can see Grandpa whenever I want. I just have to close my eyes." On a subtler level, one also sees this change to imagination at story time in the kindergarten. The younger children will usually listen to a fairy tale with their mouths open, literally drinking in the tale, tasting the sounds and feeling the rhythm of the words. The six-year-olds will often close their mouths while listening, and one can almost see the images of the story flow across their foreheads. They are clearly living into the tales in a whole new way. This aspect, coupled with the newly born memory forces, allows the school-ready children to go home and repeat in great detail the stories they heard in the kindergarten.

When teaching academics, these qualities of free memory and imagination are all important. The Waldorf first grade teacher may begin with props such as counting stones and stories about the shepherd who loses some of his sheep, but she expects the children to be able to remember what they learned yesterday and be able to add new information to the picture day after day. They need to picture their lessons inwardly and pull them out of memory as they need them. All academic learning requires these capacities, but if they are not born yet, what is the child to do? The child struggles to compensate as much as possible. Some educators say that in compensating the children learn with the cortex or covering of the brain, rather than with the deeper parts of the brain where such learning should take place. Another suggestion is made by Jane Healy in her book, *Endangered Minds*, where she surveys current brain research and suggests that more advanced learning requires nerves which are encoated with a fatty substance called myelin, which serves as an insulator and transmitter of learning. The myelinization of the sheaths, as the process is called, takes place slowly, and is not completed until early adulthood. Its rate of progress places certain organic boundaries on what can be effectively learned at different times. She says, "The relatively fixed order of myelinization in different brain areas may provide a real biological basis for 'readiness' for certain types of learning." (p.70) Jane Healy's concern is that the quality of thinking is seriously deteriorating as a result of early learning, exposure to media and other factors.

Another aspect of the mental development of first grade ready children is that they usually become interested in language arts and mathematics. This can manifest in a number of ways. Children at this stage love to play with words, make rhymes, or change the words in the songs and verses which the teacher presents in the kindergarten, and the teacher needs to find some fun materials that keep their tongues busy. They are not quite ready for tongue twisters, but verses with humor such as "My Household" in the Grimms' collection, fill them with delight. They also love learning a little bit of a foreign language, and after learning a single song or verse, will proudly go home and announce that they can speak the language in question. This is a playful door opener for the Waldorf student who will begin studying foreign languages in first grade.

A challenging aspect of this time period is that the children become interested in written language and want to be able to write their names and an assortment of words such as *Mommy, Daddy, to, from, love* and other greetings which are added to the pictures they draw for family and friends. Most children I know master ten or fifteen such words during the time before first grade and feel satisfied that they can now "read and write." In other words, at this age a little bit goes a long way. Unfortunately, often parents and educators see this budding interest and take it to mean that the child is now ready for formal instruction in written language. I have rarely seen a child who, left to his own devices, was interested in learning written language for more than a few weeks at this stage. The same is true of mathematics. The children love to play mental arithmetic with one another and will set one another challenging tasks, but one sees little interest in wanting regular practice with mathematical processes. Rather, they are at the point of "playing" with numbers and letters, and as long as they set the pace they are quite happy with it all. Only a few children I have known have actually wanted more than this playful ap-

proach, and these children taught themselves to read even though neither their parents nor their teachers wanted them to read yet. This convinced me that when the desire is strong enough, the child will overcome all barriers and learn to read, but, unfortunately, in each case it was a child who already lagged behind in social skills, and one felt that reading was going to make socializing even more difficult. It is easy for such children to place books at the center of their lives rather than human relationships.

Another aspect of mathematical thinking that awakens in many children is a interest in "infinity." One hears elaborate kindergarten conversations about this elusive concept, and one which especially struck me was between two girls, one five and one six. The five-year-old announced proudly that infinity was 6,248. The six-year-old looked scornfully at her and said, "That's not what infinity means. Infinity means *keep going.*" As a philosophy of life, it seemed admirable, and indeed during this period, the children become little philosophers. They often talk about God, creation and how the world works. Life interests them tremendously, and they are prepared to think about anything, be it cosmic or microscopic. They are far less interested in our answers than in their own, and usually are very happy if we respond to their questions by asking them what they think. They are almost always prepared to answer, and their answers are incredibly rich and full of insight.

The transition to first grade readiness is also marked by the child's leaving the world of *imitation,* which so characterizes early childhood, and entering the world of *authority.* The young child generally feels that anything the adult can do, she can do as well and is eager to participate. The school child looks at the adult as one who "knows," and views the adult as a loving authority who will dispense knowledge to the receptive child. When I assisted in a Waldorf kindergarten in Vienna, I remember a six-year-old boy who would follow me around in hopes that I would "drop" an English word on him, which I frequently did. It was clear that he looked upon me as an authority and not merely one who was to be imitated. While the children go through this important transition from imitation to authority, they frequently travel through a no-man's land where they have no sense of how to learn. They feel cut off from the learning process and express this state of being by saying, "I'm bored." This period usually lasts for a month or two, until the new phase of learning is established. During this period, one can sometimes make suggestions for play, which the children usually reject, but then replace with their own ideas. Another approach is to give the child some practical work to do. This is quite satisfying to them, and they may remain with the work for an extended period or, from the work, become inspired with a new idea for play.

There was a time when children's drawings served as a strong indicator of first grade readiness, and they still do for some children. The problem is that many children seem uncomfortable with the process of drawing and are not able to produce the archetypal pictures so closely related to the child's own growth forces. As children grow more precociously awake, it is difficult for them to draw the traditional, archetypal pictures. They are replaced with pictures of cars, ships, cartoon figures, etc. In her book, *Understanding Children's Drawings*, Michaela Strauss says:

> A comparison of the drawings that originated before the last war with the most recent ones shows that, compared with nowadays, the children at that time drew their messages more clearly. The phenomena of child development have remained the same, but the child's unconscious perception of the laws of development of his own being—which are mirrored in his drawings—appears to have become weaker. Should this fact be seen in connection with the nervousness and over-stimulation of today? (p. 10)

For children who are in touch with the archetypal forms of drawing, the signs of readiness include drawings of people whose heads, bodies and limbs are in reasonable proportion and whose feet are standing on the earth. The houses usually have square bottoms and triangle roofs, generally with an upright chimney and often with smoke emerging from it. There is usually symmetry in the picture, so if a flower appears on one side of the house, another flower will be on the other side, indicating that an awareness of the body's own symmetry has been born in the child.

An additional area of change in the school-ready children is a greater degree of sexual awareness. This is the age for "playing doctor," and children show an interest in exploring one another's bodies, especially the bodies of the opposite sex. Every parent and teacher needs to consider what message they want to impart—verbally and non-verbally—around this delicate area. Most of us do not want to impart a sense of guilt or shame around sexual exploration, but we do need to consider what the healthy boundaries are. In the kindergarten, nudity and sexual exploration in play seem inappropriate, even when they take place in play that is not sexually oriented such as when a six-year-old was "powdering" her baby by sprinkling earth and pebbles all over the four-year-old child's bare bottom. In the home, too, parents need to be clear about these boundaries when their children are playing with other children.

When all of these characteristics of change are put together, including the awakening of sexual interest, the stretching of the limbs, the awakening of the social life and of mental capacity, one finds many similarities to the changes of a youngster going into puberty and adolescence. I remember once describing the signs of first grade readiness to a group of class teachers, and the seventh grade teacher was astounded and said, "This sounds just like my class!" We call this period from around age six "the first adolescence," and it carries with it the wonder of that time of change and growth, as well as some of the pitfalls. One characteristic of adolescence is that so many changes are happening at once that it is hard for the youngster to maintain balance. They can easily become extreme, either becoming social butterflies, for example, or hermits. The same is true of children going through this first adolescence. Some want social contact all the time, some become preoccupied with the opposite sex, and some want only mental activities. The art of guiding children through this stage is to help them blossom in all areas, so that no one area becomes too lopsided.

When all of the changes are thoughtfully considered, one usually feels strongly that a child is either ready for first grade or needs to wait another year. Sometimes, however, the situation is less clear, and in such cases, my rule of thumb has been that if I am not certain, it is better to let the child wait, simply because when a child *is* ready it is so evident. Occasionally, though, one also needs to consider the relationship of the child to his classmates who are going on to first grade, or the relationship of the child to the first grade teacher. There can be the rare exception where the child is not quite ready to go on, but life circumstances dictate that it is best for the child to move forward.

Many teachers from new Waldorf initiatives which do not have grades have asked about our experience at Acorn Hill, where a number of our children have gone out to public schools at the kindergarten or first grade level. Over the years, we have seen that our students do very well when entering at the first grade level and by Christmas time have usually caught up with their classmates who have been introduced to academic subjects in kindergarten or before. We have learned that most first grade teachers need to review what the children learned in kindergarten, for at this age a great deal is forgotten over the summer. Our children enter at first grade, learn from the review period and are so fresh

and ready to learn that they take in very quickly what it took the others much longer to learn at a younger age. This process was beautifully described by a five-year-old in my kindergarten who was preparing to enter a public school kindergarten the following fall. Her sister also had been with me and had left for public kindergarten, a process I do not recommend for reasons so aptly described by this child. She was playing with some friends and said in a very serious tone, "Public kindergarten is really hard. It's *really* hard," she repeated with much emphasis. The others began looking nervous as this was clearly not what they had been told by their parents. "Yes," she went on, "it's *really, really* hard. I know because my sister told me." She paused, and in a much lighter tone added, "But first grade is easy, because you just do all the same things again!" The obvious question is: Why trouble children with academics at the kindergarten level, when it does not help and does hinder the long term learning processes?

As a practical point, when Waldorf children do need to enter non-Waldorf first grades, we have found it helpful to give a brief written description of our Waldorf kindergarten approach to the parent to pass on to the first grade teacher. We found that when the teacher realized the child had not yet been introduced to academics she viewed the child quite differently than if she assumed the child had been introduced to academics, but had retained very little. We also encouraged parents to be relaxed and supportive of the child as she went through the transition stage during the first few months of school. Children learn best if they feel this is a normal transition process and that they will soon catch on to what the teacher is asking of them. The quiet confidence of the parent is a great help.

To facilitate decisions about first grade readiness, school systems create age cut-offs. Waldorf schools also use birth dates, but generally as a guideline rather than as a strict rule. Traditionally, school systems in America used December

31 as their cut off so children under six were admitted to first grade. Many school systems have cut back to September 1 or October 1, and at least one now uses July 1. Waldorf schools have generally found that they need to cut further back than this, and many now use June 1, and a few use March 1. Classes now being formed in Waldorf schools are usually three to six months older than classes formed ten years ago, and we have heard from a number of class teachers taking a second or third class through how wonderful it is to have these older groups. They report that from the first day of school the children are ready to learn.

Questions of first grade readiness are major issues in countries that admit children into first grade at age six. In countries such as those in Scandinavia, which use age seven as the normal age for first grade, readiness is not a major issue, for nearly all seven-year-olds are ready. Where age six is used, however, the likelihood of unreadiness is so great, and the price paid by the child so enormous, that one needs to be well versed about first grade readiness in order to make the best decision for the child. Even when we consider all of changes described in this article, in the final analysis, it is knowing the child at the deepest levels that guides parents and teachers towards the right decision for that child. One hopes that the child's angel is whispering in our ear and that we are listening carefully.

Bibliography

Der Spiegel, "The Kindergarten Year," Number 20, pp. 89-90, 1977.

Elkind, David, *The Hurried Child* and *Miseducation*, Alfred Knopf, NY, 1987.

Gesell Institute publications on child development. Many titles available by Louise Bates Ames and Frances L. Ilg.

Glöckler, Michaela and Wolfgang Goebel, *A Guide to Child Health*, "When Is A Child Ready for School?" Anthroposophic Press and Floris Books, Edinburgh, 1990.

Healy, Jane, *Endangered Minds*. Simon and Schuster, NY, 1990.

Klugman, Edgar and Sara Smilansky, *Children's Play and Learning*, "Sociodramatic Play" by Sara Smilansky. Teachers College Press, NY, 1990.

Lievegoed, Bernard, *Phases of Childhood*. Floris Books and Anthroposophic Press, 1987.

Strauss, Michaela, *Understanding Children's Drawings*. Rudolf Steiner Press, London, 1978.

Uphoff, James and June Gilmore, *Summer Children*. J & J Publishing, Middletown, Ohio, 1986.

Uphoff, James and June Gilmore, "Pupil Age at School Entrance," *Educational Leadership*.

෨෮

Joan Almon is co-chair of the Waldorf Early Childhood Association of North America, is the General Secretary of the Anthrosposophical Society and is U.S. Coordinator of the Alliance for Childhood. Many of these ideas were presented in a lecture at the International Waldorf Teachers' Conference in Dornach, Switzerland, in April 1996.

Some Guidelines for First Grade Readiness

Nancy Foster

More and more often, it seems, the question of first grade readiness arises as a deep concern. The responsibility for making decisions or recommendations in this delicate area weighs heavily on many of us. As Waldorf teachers, we find that the longer we immerse ourselves in Rudolf Steiner's philosophy and the principles of Waldorf education, the better we will be able to reach wise decisions. This holds true in all aspects of our work, and earnest striving becomes an essential part of our lives.

In considering first grade readiness, we must place the child at the center of our thoughts. Guidelines for observation can be a great help, and those that follow, arranged in a somewhat rough-and-ready form, are offered in this light. No set of guidelines should be regarded as a sort of "score sheet:" if a child receives eight out of ten, "Yes, on to grade one!" On the contrary, nothing can replace the teacher's and the parents' knowledge of the individual child. It is a rare child who shows every characteristic of readiness at a given time; indeed, readiness is actually a process rather than a static point. This, of course, is where the elements of observation and experience enter in.

The parent-teacher discussion regarding readiness is an important event. In my experience, an effective approach has been first of all

to focus—teacher and parent together—on the child's needs rather than on a set of pre-conceived notions based on what "everyone else" is doing. The teacher's ability to share concrete, accurate observations of the child is a key factor here in gaining the parents' confidence. If the child's readiness is in question, it may be helpful to point out that results of a too-early placement in first grade may not show up for several years, and also that unready children do not "catch up" later on in grade school. It is useful to have some age guidelines in mind. For example, if June 1 is the cut-off date for entry into first grade, May birthdays should be looked at carefully, and in the case of boys (who generally lag about six months behind girls developmentally), even April birthdays may be questionable.

One question frequently raised by parents is that of intellectual readiness: "My child is so eager to learn letters and numbers. Shouldn't he go on to first grade?" Parents fear that if instruction does not begin, the child might be frustrated or the interest atrophy. A child, however, may show interest in letters and numbers quite early—even at age four or five—and may want to copy letters, or may ask how to spell words, etc. This interest may arise naturally out of imitation of the parents or older children. In itself, it is not necessarily a sign of intellectual readiness, and often dies away before reawakening when the child is really ready for first grade. In any case, a child who is truly ready to read will learn to do so, one way or another, even without instruction. Intellectual and emotional readiness may develop at different rates, and intellectual readiness alone is not an adequate reason for placement in first grade.

In talking with parents of a child whose readiness is in doubt, it is useful if the teacher is able to describe what that particular child would gain from another year in kindergarten. Parents may wonder whether the year would simply be a repetition, and the teacher can explain that a child takes from an experience what she is ready for—that watercolor painting, for example, will be experienced very differently by a four-year-old and a six-year-old. It is especially important, however, that the parents be helped to feel confident that the teacher will not simply repeat the same activities and stories year after year, but that, instead, the program will be planned according to the needs of a particular group of children. The teacher will keep in mind the needs of the older, almost-ready-for-first-grade children, and make sure that they are offered experiences to challenge them and help them grow—still without pushing. The teacher can also help the parents consider their child's readiness by asking them to picture the child in a first grade setting (always realizing, of course, that several months are yet to pass) and with the children who will be in the first grade group.

There is some risk in keeping a child in kindergarten too long, if the child has really reached the stage at which first grade activities are appropriate. Such a situation might arise, for example, in a school where there is not yet a first grade, and the parent wishes the child to remain in kindergarten one more year until a first grade is begun. Or it might arise if the teacher or parent is overly cautious. In this case, the needs of the child will not be met, and unhappiness or discipline problems may arise. It seems fairly clear, however, that there is more likelihood of error

on the side of too-early placement than too-late, and many teachers feel: "When in doubt—wait!" Particularly in today's society, with its emphasis on acceleration in education, we must counteract the pressures to move children ahead too soon. There may also be a situation in which it must be determined whether a child needs another year of kindergarten even though he or she is chronologically ready, or whether there may be a developmental problem that needs to be addressed.

A teacher need not feel ashamed to be unsure about a child's placement. It is best to be open with the parents, and to share with them those areas in question which they can observe for themselves. In this way the parents will feel comfortable about expressing their own questions openly and honestly, and a mutually helpful dialogue can take place. Parents will appreciate feeling that they have shared in the thinking process that leads to a recommendation.

Teachers and parents need to be clear about who it is that makes the final placement decision in questionable cases. Depending on the particular school, this will vary: Is it the faculty chairman? The College of Teachers? The incoming first grade teacher? The school doctor? The kindergarten teacher? The parents? It is a good idea to establish this clearly, as well as the procedures and timetable for reaching a decision. This will be especially helpful in cases when the kindergarten teacher and parents may not see eye-to-eye or there is a communication difficulty. Ideally, there will be mutual trust and confidence, but unfortunately this cannot always be the case, and then parents and teachers—like their children—need firm guidelines!

The following guidelines obviously are not to be brought to the attention of the children in question! They are based on information gained from various sources, including Margret Meyerkort, Elisabeth Moore-Haas, Bronja Zahlingen, and the Waldorf Institute (now Sunbridge College), as well as my own and colleagues' observations. Since some of the information is "secondhand," and it has not been possible to check it all with its sources, teachers should be aware that there is the possibility of error or misinterpretation in spite of well-meant efforts to be accurate. In addition, this is certainly not presented as a complete, definitive list and, once again, it is not to be used as a checklist or score sheet, but rather as an aid to observation. For this reason, the guidelines include, in some parts, more than simply readiness characteristics, but also indicate preliminary stages, which may help give a broader perspective.

With these reservations and qualifications, the guidelines are offered in the hope that they will help kindergarten teachers to know their children better.

Physical Development

1. **Bodily proportions and characteristics:** Individual differences due to body type must be considered. In general, the head: body ratio changes from about 1:4 in infancy, to 1:6 at age seven, to 1:8 in the adult. These numbers mean that the head of the adult is 1/8 of the total body length, including the head. (See Lievegoed, Phases of Childhood.) Loss of baby fat and the "pot belly" should occur toward the end of the fifth year. The "first stretching" (growth of the legs) should occur toward the end of the sixth year. A school-ready child should have developed:

   a. Ability to touch top of ear by reaching over top of head with opposite arm.

   b. Waist and neck incisions in the trunk, indicating that the rhythmic system is maturing and becoming ready for first grade instruction

   c. Visible joints (knuckles) and kneecaps instead of dimples

   d. Arch in foot

   e. Individualized facial features instead of baby features (child who has not been able to undergo childhood illnesses may be hindered in this development)

   f. S-curve in spine

2. **Second dentition:** Usually a first-grade-ready child should have at least a loose tooth. If one or both parents, however, were slow in reaching second dentition, this factor should not be weighed as heavily for the particular child. The appearance of the 6-year molars is also a factor to be observed.

3. **Physical abilities:** The school-ready child should be able to do many or most of the following, as observed in spontaneous play (a child should not be "tested" on these items!):

   a. Walk a beam, log, (or line) forward

   b. Catch and throw a large ball

   c. Hop on either foot

   d. Bunny hop (both feet together)

   e. Habitually walk in cross pattern (i.e. swing opposite arm when stepping out with one foot)

   f. Climb stairs with alternating feet on each stair

   g. Tie knots or, sometimes, bows; button; zip own clothing

   h. Use fingers dexterously (sew, finger knit, play finger games, etc.)

   i. Have established dominance (eye/hand dominance most important)—though this may in some cases not be firmly established until age nine

   j. Not be unduly restless or lethargic

   k. Shake hands with thumb separated from fingers, rather than offering the whole hand

Social and Emotional Development

1. The following stages can be observed in play:

a. Age two–three: not really social; wants to possess and try out; reactive, transitory feelings

b. Ages three–four: begins a bit to discover the "other," but still self-centered; beginning of fantasy stage (transforms objects to meet own needs); activity for its own sake, not goal-oriented; or, transitory, quickly-changing goals (play with wood pieces may result in a house, which then becomes a campfire, etc., all without planning ahead)

c. Age five: real need for social experience; beginning of give-and-take, sharing; some beginnings of planning in play

d. School-ready child: develops feeling for others' needs—social awareness, doing things for others; goal-oriented play—planning, thinking things out; does not need objects in play (can now "visualize" play rather than needing to collect many items as younger children did; this shows separation of concept/inner world from percept/outer world); begins more long-term friendships; play of horses and dogs (shows readiness for authority of first grade, obeying a "master")

2. Other social/emotional abilities of the school-ready child:

a. Ability to join in offered activities

b. Ability to look after own eating, drinking, washing, toileting needs

c. Ability to share teacher's or parent's attention and wait for a turn

d. Ability to follow instructions and carry through with a task or activity

e. Not be unduly dependent on a "security item" (thumb, blanket, etc.)

f. Not be regularly the aggressor or victim; be accepted by most other children

Drawing and Painting (Don't wait for all aspects to appear for any one child.)

1. Development of the will—shown in stages similar to those in play:

a. Activity for its own sake

Drawing: Child is involved in the movement, gesture of the activity. Spirals, zig-zags.

Painting: Process is paramount; stage of water, "mud," and possible scratches from vigorous gesture.

b. Fantasy stage

Drawing: Child's fantasy is caught up by the activity; child's identification of an object in his drawing seems to arise out of the activity ("Oh, and here is a bear!" rather than "Now I'll draw a bear.")

Painting: unconscious, flowing beauty of colors.

c. School-ready child

Drawing: conscious goal in drawing picture.

Painting: Child becomes goal-conscious, attempts forms or "special effects" such as dots; paintings become stiffer, less beautiful for a time, but may then free up again later as child consciously discovers how to mix and blend colors and develops designs or forms appropriate to the medium; symmetrical designs, similar to crayon drawings, may appear.

2. Content of pictures (primarily in drawing):

a. Evolution of human form: circle; then circle with eyes; then circle with appendages; then trunk is developed. Most mature form of trunk is triangular. Addition of fingers and other details.

b. Change in emphasis from line (youngest children) to surface and color (older children want to color in objects, perhaps give people patterned clothing, etc.)

c. School-ready child:

1. Two-fold symmetry, indicating that the two-fold function of the brain has come about: symmetrical houses, often with a tree or flower on each side; or symmetrical designs in which the paper is divided into halves or quarters, often diagonally

2. Symmetrical color arrangements.

3. "Change-of-teeth" pictures, containing horizontal repetitions such as birds flying, rows of mountains, etc., reminiscent of rows of teeth.

4. Strip of sky and earth, showing child's awareness of "above and below" rather than the younger child's feeling of wholeness.

5. Use of the diagonal (related to brain development). Frequently seen in triangle form of roof or in drawing of stairs.

6. People and houses resting on grass at bottom of page.

Soul Life (Thinking, Feeling, Willing)

1. Signs of first grade readiness in the will:

a. Conscious goals appear in play, drawing, painting, handwork; consciousness of self as creator results in awareness of the distinction between inner (desire) and outer (result). At "first puberty" this leads to the characteristic feelings of loneliness and inability (which may be expressed as "I'm bored"). This is an important stage, as it leads to the basis for natural respect which is to be found in the grade school years—the realization by the child that there are some things he can't yet do as well as the adult.

b. Use of limbs is vigorous, active; the child likes to move furniture and heavy stumps, and use all available play cloths.

c. The child likes to run errands (again, goal consciousness).

2. Signs of first grade readiness in the feeling life:

a. Stormy period of first puberty proceeding to more calm; can handle feelings better; needs less adult intervention.

b. Wrapping of objects as gifts (child "wraps himself around" the object).

c. Loves humor, limericks, rhymes, play on words, silly words.

d. May say verse faster than rest of group, or hold note longer at end of song (is beginning to grow aware in the realm of rhythm).

e. Likes to whisper, have secrets (distinction between inner and outer).

f. May like to tell of dreams (soul has made a step inward); awareness of inner and outer life. (Be careful this isn't imitation of adults or just telling a story; and don't question children about dreams.)

3. Signs of first grade readiness in the thinking/cognitive realm:

a. Development of causal thinking ("if," "because," "therefore;" for example, "If I tie these strings together, they will reach that play stand," and also in the wish to tie things together with yarn, "tying" thoughts together in causal thinking).

b. Correct use of verb tenses ("I stood," not "I standed.")

c. Enjoys cunning, planning, and scheming.

d. Enjoys humor and making up or repeating simple riddles, (typical for this age mentality is, "Why was the cook mean?" "Because he beat the eggs and whipped the cream.") It is best that the teacher not introduce real riddles at this stage; they are appropriate for older children.

e. Memory becomes conscious; child can, at will or upon request, repeat stories and songs with accuracy

f. Speaks fluently and clearly and can express ideas easily and fully.

g. Can concentrate on a chosen task for ten to fifteen minutes.

h. Image-formation: is no longer dependent on objects in play, but can visualize (e.g. may build a house and then, instead of collecting dishes, food, etc., may simply "talk through" the play). Conversations and discussions among the children become important to them.

i. Appearance of "real" questions (not the typical younger child's constant "why," or questions for the sake of asking).

Factors in Borderline Cases

1. Boys are generally about six months behind girls in level of maturity at this age.

2. Unreadiness for first grade may manifest itself in the early grades as lack of stamina and concentration, and difficulty in keeping up with the rhythmical work, or with games and handwork.

3. Younger children may be left behind socially; this usually becomes apparent toward the end of third grade, and may become more marked during the change at age twelve.

4. If there is any academic difficulty, it will be exacerbated if the child enters first grade as a younger child, and reading problems may become severe. On the other hand, if the child is held back, he may later excel.

5. If a child is always youngest in the class, he may never have the opportunity to become a leader. ("Leader" here means not "the boss," but one who has the inner strength and security to be an example to others and bring out the best in them.)

6. The composition of the first grade group should be considered: How will this child fit in, both socially and chronologically? Is it a "young" class or an "old" one, for example?

☙

Nancy Foster has been a Waldorf kindergarten teacher since 1973 at Acorn Hill Waldorf Kindergarten and Nursery in Silver Spring, Maryland where she now works with parents and children in parent/child groups. She also lectures, offers workshops for Waldorf kindergarten teachers, and is on the visiting faculty of Sunbridge College in Spring Valley, New York. She is the author and editor of Let Us Form a Ring *and* Dancing as We Sing. *She and her husband, a professional musician, encountered Waldorf education and Anthroposophy while seeking a school for their two sons, now grown.*

92356022R00080

Made in the USA
San Bernardino, CA
01 November 2018